To Karl and Louise

My Parents

for helping me to learn

that love

can explain some things

even economics can't explain

The economic problem, the struggle for subsistence, always has been hitherto the primary, most pressing problem of the human race—not only of the human race, but of the whole of the biological kingdom from the beginnings of life in its most primitive forms.

Thus we have been expressly evolved by nature—with all our impulses and deepest instincts—for the purpose of solving the economic problem.

—Lord John Maynard Keynes

Economics
Deciphered

ECONOMICS DECIPHERED

A Layman's Survival Guide

MAURICE LEVI

Basic Books, Inc., Publishers NEW YORK

Library of Congress Cataloging in Publication Data

Levi, Maurice D   1945–
  Economics deciphered.
  Bibliography: p. 279
  Includes index.
  1. Economics.   I.   Title.
HB171.L635   330   80–68173
ISBN: 0–465–01794–0

CONTENTS

III

THE ECONOMICS OF CONSUMERS AND FIRMS

IV

INTERNATIONAL ECONOMICS AND EXCHANGE RATES

V

THE ECONOMISTS AND THEIR BOOKS

PREFACE

This book is for the bewildered—those who are not sure what or whom to believe. It explains in clear, straightforward terms what an educated person should know about economics. It takes nothing for granted and provides consistent answers to the important questions. After reading these pages, you should have sufficient knowledge of economics to understand the environment around you and to make sensible personal and professional decisions to survive and prosper in that environment. You will know what you should know and when you are being "put on" by somebody who doesn't know.

If you thumb through the pages, what you will find is a wide variety of questions and answers. By taking this approach, we are able to quickly answer the economic questions that are important to everyone. Every person embarking upon an introduction to economics, whether self-directed or in a course offered in a school or college, wants and deserves speedy rewards. The greatest reward of learning is discovering the answers to what has been puzzling. This is most quickly achieved in a question and answer format.

This book contains no graphs or mathematics. An understanding of economics requires nothing but common sense—and a good book. There is absolutely nothing in these pages that cannot be understood by an average, interested, intelligent human being. You have revealed sufficient interest by beginning this book. All that remains is to use your intelligence.

The intention is to provide the reader with enough self-confidence to participate comfortably in conversations about economic matters. You can avoid that uneasy and queasy feeling that sometimes occurs when conversations shift to subjects on which you feel uninformed. In doing so, you will find that economics is an exciting and dynamic discipline and that those who try to escape conversations about economics do so more out of fear of revealing what they *don't* know than because of what they already *do* know. When it comes to learning, what you don't know can hurt you. It can prevent you from learning about the powerful forces shaping your personal and national economic survival.

An author's debts are a pleasure to acknowledge and I am fortunate in having incurred many. I owe special debts that I could never repay to the Faculty of Commerce of the University of British Columbia, the University of California, Berkeley, the National Bureau of Economic Research, and the Massachusetts Institute of Technology. All provided pleasant and stimulating environments while this book evolved. The enthusiasm and professional advice of Martin Kessler and his editorial staff have helped me survive revisions to numerous drafts, and Ellen McGibbon has stoically typed the manuscript. But it is to Kate Birkinshaw that I owe my greatest debt for her patience and cheerfulness while I indulged in the joy of writing this book.

I

Introducing Economics

1

THE NATURE
OF ECONOMICS:
AN OVERVIEW

Survival itself can depend on economics.

Paul Samuelson
Nobel Laureate in Economics

What questions does economics answer?

Economics is concerned with answering questions about
inflation and unemployment, the stock market, gold prices,
and the foreign-exchange value of the dollar. It is concerned
with national income, interest rates, the market price of oil,
and the rewards of labor and investment. With such a vast
area covered, it is no wonder that many otherwise informed
laymen are perplexed by economic events around them.
Adding to the sense of confusion is the disagreement among
economists. We hear different views from monetarists and
Keynesians, from those in favor of free enterprise and those
supporting government intervention, and from other oppos-
ing camps.

Even when economists find themselves in agreement,
their conclusions frequently seem to have been arrived at

with mirrors. We discover, for example, that when robber barons burn money at lavish, ostentatious dinner parties to show off their wealth, they are making a gift to the rest of us; and that high interest rates follow easy, not tight, money-supply policy. We discover that while as individuals, the best way to prepare for unemployment is to increase savings, for the nation as a whole, savings should be decreased; and we discover that poor harvests can make farmers richer. These conclusions, as well as others more in line with common sense need deciphering. But is it worthwhile to find the answers?

Why should we decipher economics?

Economics is important for survival. It helps to explain, for example, the forces that put food on our dinner tables, even in a largely urbanized society. By a remarkably smooth running system, food and other vital items from around the world are produced, processed, wholesaled, distributed, and made available in local stores. Economics drives the productive wheels of society, and the more people who understand the energy behind these wheels, the more likely we are to maintain the momentum of a productive economy. Informed decisions by the public at large, in the voting booth and in daily life, will help ensure that we do not damage the marvelous machinery that is the economic system.

Understanding economics is important in helping us face personal choices. If we can chart the course of the general economy, we can make wiser choices in careers, in business ventures, and in future savings and spending plans. Charting the course of the economy requires that we understand the business press and the decisions and claims of government. Economic literacy will help us decide not only what we ourselves can afford, but what the nation can afford in terms of military expenditures, security for the old, housing, medicine, and other government programs. By helping us to make informed and wise choices, an appreciation of economics can enable us to survive as individuals, and to prosper as new economic opportunities unfold.

What makes choice so important?

The reason why choice is necessary in our personal lives—between a new car and a stereo, between beef and fish for the evening meal—is because good things are scarce. This is the same reason why government must choose between the military and welfare—or between guns and butter—and why, if democracy is to survive, we, the public, must ultimately make the choice for government.

So important is scarcity to economics that the subject is often defined as the study of choice in the face of scarcity. This doesn't mean just diamonds and gold and famous works of art, although economics is concerned with the value of these things. It means anything for which there is a price or cost. All the food, clothing, housing, transportation, entertainment, and everything else we buy for enjoyment or from necessity has a price, and these prices and amounts are studied by economists. But there is also a cost in having a family and deciding on its size, and so even our very private behavior has not escaped the scrutiny of the economist. Maintaining clean air and water is costly, and economists therefore study the environment. Costs occur whenever products are in short supply.

What is in short supply?

Our expectations are constantly growing. Most people want a comfortable home, a reliable car, an adequate supply of good food and clothing, and even a television or a stereo. This is what most of us want, but it is not what everybody has. And even those who do have these things feel that they could enjoy having just a little bit more. It is because our wants seem to always move ahead of what we have that there is never quite enough of everything to go around. Putting this a little differently, outputs are always scarce.

Limits on outputs—food, homes, cars, TVs and stereos—are themselves the result of limits on inputs that are available to produce them. It takes inputs of human effort, raw material, land, and machines to produce outputs we want and need. But there are only so many human hands, barrels of oil, tons of steel, acres of land, and productive machines. If we use more people and machines to build automobiles, then there are less of these available to help satisfy our other needs. If we grow more corn and wheat by allocating a larger amount of land and people, fertilizers and farm machines, we will have less output of other products, such as barley or soy beans. The scarcity of inputs accounts for the short supply of outputs. Technology has helped us make much better use of what we have, but it is never likely to completely bridge the gap between our wants and our ability to produce. With that gap unclosed, the economist must continue to approach the economic problem.

What is the economic approach?

Economists take a scientific approach, which involves setting up theories based on assumptions and constantly testing these theories. The fact that, like other social sciences, economics is somewhat imprecise, does not preclude the application of scientific methods to it. There are some physical sciences that have seen a sufficient number of rejected theories and hypotheses that, on the level of precision, it would be difficult to distinguish them from some social sciences. The scientific nature of economics goes beyond the methods that are used. Even the topics covered in economics are similar to those found in natural sciences, with the most notable similarities being those between biology and economics.

Specialization of tasks is central to the study of biology and economics. In the economy, people hopefully concentrate on working at what they do best. Smart people become physicians, strong people become loggers, creative people become artists, and patient people become teachers of economics. And all parts of nature demonstrate specialization, with each part of a whole doing the job for which it is best suited. Leaves collect light and stems carry water. Back teeth chew and front teeth bite. There are also divisions of labor within social insects. Ants are divided into those who work and those who go to war, and among bees the queen specializes in reproduction. All species show survival of the fittest in a competitive environment, and humans are not unique in dividing up their labor and sharing their cooperative efforts. Nor are economists unique in approaching their problems with models.

What is an economic "model"?
Can I see it and play with it?

You can't see a model. A model is just a term that describes the economist's view of how he believes things work. It has no physical being. Sorry to disappoint you, but economists are not having that much fun when they stay late at the office to play with their models. At least I am not.

A good model is one that describes the way the world runs, at least for that part of the world it purports to explain. For example, a good model of national income should explain why national income changes as it does. A good macroeconomic model should explain national income, unemployment, inflation, interest rates, and other macroeconomic variables. Economists frequently use mathematics in their models to simplify things. Mathematics helps them keep track of all the parts of their model, but, in general, a model does *not* have to be mathematical.

What types of models are there?

There are macroeconomic models, worldwide econometric models, and microeconomic models. There are small models of supply and demand and models of the demand for frozen Brussels sprouts. Really. No kidding. There are models of the whole U.S. economy and some models of the whole world. There are energy-supply models and ones for energy demand. Just about everything of interest—and more—has been modeled by someone.

The big models that involve hundreds of mathematical equations and are built by the government or some major university—at the government's expense—tend to use computers. What is common to all models, whether they use computers or are just in the mind of the economist, is the need to make assumptions.

What can an economist assume?

Economists are artists when it comes to making assumptions. They can assume just about anything and, indeed, some time ago a professional "in" joke for economists ran like this: A brilliant theoretical physicist, an engineer, and an economist were marooned and starving. They had a can of beans but no can opener. The theoretical physicist examined the can and computed, with sophisticated mathematics, the weakest point in a cylindrical structure at which to begin applying pressure. The engineer hunted for an appropriately sharp object with which to strike the can. The economist said, "Assume a can opener . . ."

Economists are forever assuming, in a world that is constantly in dynamic motion, that "everything else is unchanged and equal." This assumption is sometimes hidden in a Latin phrase—*ceteris paribus*—in the hope that others will not understand what is being slipped in. Sometimes they will "assume there is no government," or "imagine a world with no taxes." This is not a descrition of their ideal utopian economy but an assumption that is necessary for their argument. But making assumptions is not necessarily a bad thing.

What makes a good assumption?

Ours is a complicated world. To describe this world in a manner we can comprehend, we must forgo some of the detail of the real world. It's rather like comparing a photograph to a pencil sketch. A good artist can, in just a few strokes, give a very good impression of a person's face, or perhaps a scene of a man on a horse, or a graceful flower. Some of the line drawings of Rembrandt, or even lesser-known artists, are remarkable for their rendering of complex subjects with so few lines and such minimal shading. Virtually all the detail that might have been made is missing, yet the viewer has a truly good image of what is to be seen.

This is why a good economist must be an artist at using assumptions. He must prune away the unnecessary detail and leave only the essence. If the wrong lines have been used and the discarded detail was really of value, what he is left with will not be a useful image. A good sketch—and an economist's model—should be judged by how well it describes the subject. If the assumptions that were made yield a model that explains things well, then this is what counts. We might, to take an example, assume that we need not look at specific conditions in the beef, newsprint, and other individual markets when explaining what causes inflation or unemployment, even though the individual markets are part of the overall picture. Or we might assume that we need not look at unemployment rates in explaining the price of beef. As long as these assumptions allow us to explain, in a straightforward fashion, what we wish to explain, then they are good assumptions. A good assumption is one that eliminates as much real detail as possible and retains the valuable explanatory power in the theory or model.

To take an example from another area of study, we might assume that the earth is flat. We all know that the earth is not flat, although the Flat Earth Society does boast a membership that reaches into double figures. Yet, in calculating the distance from our front door to the nearest grocery store, we are unlikely to go far wrong by ignoring the arc of the curvature of the earth. An accurate prediction of traveling distance that is made from a good local map is not seriously affected by the assumption of a flat world—an assumption that enters into a large part of map making. The assumption avoids great complication and gives an accurate picture of the part of the world being described, provided that part is small. In maps of the entire globe, however, a flat earth can be a very misleading approximation if the purpose is to compute distance. Evaluate an economist's assumption in the same way, by his purpose and the realism of his final result.

In judging the final result, the economist calls in the services of an econometrician. An econometrician is an economist who specializes in the statistical field of econometrics.

What is involved in econometrics?

Econometrics is the branch of economics that uses historical events to test which theory comes closest to explaining what happened. The historical events take the form of statistical measurement of the economic variables in the economist's model, such as prices, incomes, interest rates, money supplies, stock prices, and so on. The economist then asks the computer: Given this information on the way the world has been in the past (perhaps in terms of inflation, unemployment, and so on), *and* given the model I've constructed, please fill in the bits of the model I didn't know and then tell me if the theory is or isn't untrue.

But can an economist tell if a theory is untrue?

An economist or even an econometrician can never prove a theory to be definitely true, which is probably why there are as many theories as there are economists. I have even heard tell that there are more theories than economists. That's why they'll let you hear them. They are often not worth too much; there's an oversupply. But while he can't prove a theory to be definitely true, the econometrician can show which theories are untrue and, in this manner, come nearer to knowing how economies work.

What specializations exist within economics?

The two larger areas in which economists specialize are known as microeconomics—concerned with consumers and firms—and macroeconomics—concerned with the overall economy. But even within both microeconomics and macroeconomics there are many further subspecializations. There are mathematical economists, econometricians, and theoreticians. There are those who are expert in public finance, personal finance, agricultural economics, and the economics of underdevelopment. There are labor-market economists, energy economists, money and banking economists, financial economists, and more.

Axel Leijonhufvud (whose surname I can't help you pronounce, but I can tell you that it means "lion's head" in Norwegian) once described the life among a tribe called the "Econ" as if he were returning from an anthropological field trip. The Econ, he said, were split into two major divisions—the Micro-Econ and the Macro-Econ. Within each division there were a variety of castes. At the top sat the Math-Econ, and down at the end were the Devlops (economists concerned with the problems of underdeveloped nations and for whom words are a common means of conveying their beliefs; the Math-Econ on the other hand, avoid words whenever they can). Anyway, those in the higher castes never spoke to the Polscis (political scientists) or the Sociogs (sociologists), although the Devlops had been known to associate with them. And we can add that no Econ, even a Devlop, ever dreamed of talking with a Home-Econ. Home-Econ study effectively planned housekeeping and how to bake good pie, and in adding the "economics" to their name they have confused the public. For their part, economists can tell you about the national pie, but they know only how to enjoy the ones made with apples and served with ice cream.

To become an elder, or "prof," in the Econ tribe, the younger Econ, called "grads," were required to manufacture a "modl" (an economic model, which is his stock in trade). The more ornate the modl, the higher the caste that the grad could enter.

It is time that we entered the Land of the Econ to learn more of their habits and language. Since they are so specialized, we will first meet the Macro-Econ and will start by explaining what they do in their mysterious land, which is visited by so few people from the outside.

II

The Economics of
the Nation

2

DEFINING
UNEMPLOYMENT,
INFLATION,
NATIONAL INCOME . . .

Every short statement about economics is misleading (with the possible exception of my present one).

Alfred Marshall

What is a cynic? A man who knows the price of everything and the value of nothing.

Oscar Wilde

What is macroeconomics and how does it differ from microeconomics?

Macroeconomics is concerned with the economy as a whole. It is concerned with the national income, the nation's rate of unemployment and inflation, the level of national savings, and the like. Microeconomics, on the other hand, is concerned with the individual consumers and firms that make up the economy and the prices of individual products. It is concerned with such questions as why beef prices rise when herds have been reduced, and why produce prices fall after good harvests. It is concerned with how consumers adjust the amounts they buy to prices, and what we need to know to maximize profits or to get the most satisfaction from spending a dollar.

Macroeconomics and microeconomics are the two major divisions of the subject matter of economics—the big, or macro-scale, issues and the small, or micro-scale, issues. We will start out by worrying about the economy as a whole and will ask some big questions you might always have wanted to ask. The answers to these questions will reveal that no question should embarrass you. Even questions that appear to be ridiculously obvious turn out to be not so obvious after all. For example:

What is full employment?

Well, it's obviously not everybody being employed. Babies, ninety-year-olds, women who are about to undergo birth-associated labor, and prisoners under maximum security are not expected to work, nor are they able to. How about saying that full employment is when all able-bodied people are working? Again, this is too broad. High-school seniors, college students, mothers who wish to remain at home with their families (or fathers who switch roles to stay at home)— these are presumably able-bodied people, but we wouldn't call them unemployed. Let's stop here. It won't help to go any further. Clearly, we should change our tack to produce a useful definition. How about this: "All people who would like a job with a job." Closer, but we still have problems. In any healthy economy we have people between jobs, if only because we live in an open society where people like to explore other opportunities. (One guess at why Soviet unemployment figures are so low!) Other people are displaced because demand for some products and services declines while demand for others rise. This is part and parcel of a dynamic world. What we can do to take care of these small problems is to say this: "Full employment is where only x percent (say, 5 or even 6 percent) of the people who would like a job are looking for a job." The number looking for jobs is determined in a monthly survey taken by the Census Bureau. The survey covers about 50,000 households and asks what people were doing last week. If they did not work but were actively looking for work, they are counted as unemployed.

This search for a definition tells us something that's most important. Never be afraid to ask even the simplest-appearing question about economics. People throw words and concepts around as if everyone else agrees on their meaning. There's little in economics on which many economists agree, at least in public. I even heard one skeptical leading economist say that if we gave x economists a problem, they would produce at least $x + 1$ answers. For this reason, be especially dubious about any economist who says, "It's obvious . . ." This is a sure sign that it isn't. Even "facts" can turn out to be misleading and wrong. Take, for example, a question all of us feel we can answer through experience:

What is inflation?

To some people, inflation just means that their checks bounce higher. More accurately, inflation is the rate at which prices in general are increasing per year (and deflation is the rate at which they are decreasing). The only problem is defining what we mean by prices in general. We have a couple of ways to proceed, but most commonly we use the consumer price index, the CPI.

What is the Consumer Price Index?

The consumer price index is a gauge by which we can measure the cost of living for a representative consumer. Indeed, it is often known as a cost-of-living index. As a first step in preparing this index, official Labor Department surveyors are sent out about once every ten years to determine what it is that urban households are buying. (It is assumed that urban households are the typical households.) For example, they may find that, of its total budget, a family spends 25 percent on rent, 20 percent on food, 8 percent on heat and utilities, 6 percent on gas, 5 percent on clothes, 2 percent on eating out, 2 percent on health, 1 percent on bus rides, and so on. In even greater detail they check the food budget; how much is spent on meat, eggs, produce, cereals, and certain brands of items, such as cleaning aids. The average of the fractions spent on the different items in the budgets of a large number of similar urban households, when averaged over these households, gives an idea of the representative or typical household or consumer. Some of the households the surveyors use might have an extravagant taste for caviar and lox. Others might indulge excessively in bologna. But by averaging the fractions spent on different items by a large number of households, the surveyors get an idea of the normal or representative budget.

Once the representative consumer's budget has been defined—what we call establishing the base—the next step is to price the same combination of items each and every month. As closely as possible, the surveyors try to keep the base that they have set—even down to finding the cost of a large tube of Crest toothpaste in a discount drugstore. By finding the cost of the base every month, the surveyors can compare the general price change between months. The rate at which prices in general are changing is the rate of inflation, but notice that the spending pattern of the representative consumer should be recalculated every so often, say, each ten years. We can't keep assuming that someone persists in guzzling gas when gas prices skyrocket or that he or she still buys hair grease when it goes out of style. The longer it is since our representative consumer household was resurveyed, the poorer the consumer price index will be when it is used.

How is the CPI used?

We should not leave the CPI before pointing out some different ways in which it is used. Sometimes you will hear that "consumer prices increased by half a percentage point last month, an annual rate of inflation of 6 percent." Note that the 6 percent will be accurate only if this situation were to persist for the next eleven months. At other times you will hear, "Consumer prices increased by a half a percent last month, bringing inflation for the last twelve months to 10 percent." On still other occasions, you might hear that consumer prices increased by half a percentage point last month, bringing the year's inflation (meaning since January, *not* for the last twelve months) to 7 percent. Even more frequently, the information conveyed is just that the new CPI shows an inflation rate of 6 percent, 10 percent, or 7 percent, without any explanation of what that means. Yet we see that all these different figures are consistent with a one-half percent increase in the CPI over the previous month. Since writers and broadcasters and economists, in general, are likely to use the "fact" that most clearly supports their case, we see that we must be careful in drawing conclusions from these facts. An even more important problem concerns the possible incorrect measurement of inflation given by the CPI.

What CPI measurement errors exist?

Problems in interpreting the CPI can be overcome. We have to learn how to use the statistics properly and then, with care, we can learn what they mean. But if the statistics themselves are wrong and can give false readings, they will provide the wrong answers, however much care we exercise in using them. Although it is not generally known outside of relatively narrow economic circles, the CPI does involve an essential flaw and generally overstates the rate of inflation. A little careful examination will show us how this happens.

We have explained how, in the construction of the CPI, the government calculates the fraction of the total family budget than an average or representative household spends on each item in the base year. But because the supply and demand of the various items in this basket change at different rates, some prices rise more and some less. Some prices even decline. These are relative price changes to which the typical consumer responds by changing what he or she buys. For example, in the spring, when strawberry prices fall, more are bought than in the winter when strawberries—if available at all—are high priced because they are flown in from distant places. Similarly, when home heating oil prices rise more rapidly than natural gas prices, more new houses use gas, and some of the older homes are even converted to the relatively cheaper fuel. So we discover that as relative prices go up, people buy less, and as relative prices go down, they buy more. This causes the CPI to overstate inflation.

How does the CPI overstate inflation?

As we have said, the fractions of the representative consumer's budget for different items, called weights, are only infrequently revised. In fact, since we are still using the 1967 base we are working with weights (with some small revisions) that were determined by average buying patterns more than ten years in the past. But people change their buying patterns as relative prices go up and down. People buy less of goods whose prices go up and more of those whose prices go down. The new true weights that should be used should therefore be smaller on the items that registered a sizable price increase (because less are bought) and larger on those that carry more modest price increases (because more are bought).

To take an example, in 1967 it was not uncommon to purchase silverware because silver was relatively affordable. Silver prices increased rapidly in the 1970s, and the purchase of silverware became rarer. If we used the amount of silverware purchased by a representative consumer in 1967 to compute the cost of living for 1980, we would be attaching too much importance to silverware. In 1980 a smaller quantity was purchased than in the base year of 1967 and it should therefore have a smaller weight in the price index. However, by using the relatively large 1967 weights, the 1980 CPI is higher than it should be. The rate of inflation, using 1967 standards, is thus also higher than it should be.

Just as the old weights are too large on items whose prices went up rapidly, the old weights are too small on those items that have experienced a more moderate price increase. The index provided by the CPI therefore gives an upward-biased indication of inflation. By failing to take account of how consumers adapt to higher prices by moving out of relatively higher-priced items into those with relatively lower prices, the CPI overstates the amount of inflation that "really" occurred. That doesn't make big inflation figures a welcome event, but it could make them more tolerable.

The CPI also fails to consider new commodities that have been introduced since the base was calculated. It also takes no careful account of changes in quality.

The CPI is not the only price index that is published. This causes more potential problems in determining *the* rate of inflation.

What other price indexes are published?

We also hear each month of the *producer price index*, which is also called *the wholesale price index (WPI)*. This is an index constructed somewhat like the CPI, but for prices at the wholesale level. It is not relevant for what we, the consumers, buy, but note that since wholesale goods are eventually processed and end up in the stores, what happens to wholesale or producer prices now will probably affect consumer prices later. Another price index published in the government's national income account statistics is known as a *deflator*. This is given only four times a year and does not receive as much attention as the CPI or the WPI, even though it is a very good index and includes the price of everything produced.

Inflation is important because of what it does to the buying power of our incomes which, in macroeconomics, means our national income. The nation's income goes under several names and several guises. We probably feel we should know what people mean by the gross national product, national income, gross national expenditures, real income and the associated growth rates, and so on, but we might have been too embarrassed to ask or believed it would all be too difficult to understand. Well, the concepts are easy, so let's ask the questions now.

What is the Gross National Product?

The gross national product (or GNP) is simply the value of all the goods and services produced within the nation during a calendar year. This includes the value of everything, not just of consumer goods. We add the value of cars, apples, new houses, new machines, dry-cleaning bills, theater tickets, new books, newspapers, toilet seats, toothpaste, and so on. This suggests the question:

But how do you add toothpaste to toilet seats?

Remember that we are adding *values* of items produced. If the nation produced 1 million new toilet seats at an average final price of $20 each, that's $20 million. We add this to the value of toothpaste produced, which might be 200 million tubes at an average price of $2, giving $400 million. We just keep adding the values of all the goods and services produced during the year.

*Is the value of absolutely everything included
in the GNP?*

To be included, goods must be new, be in their final stage
of fabrication, and be produced in our own country. Let's be
more specific. If a ten-year-old house changed hands during
the year, it isn't new and is therefore not part of this year's
national product. A used car isn't either.

If a hardwood merchant sells fine hardwoods to a furniture manufacturer who then produces and sells furniture,
the nation's product does not include the wood sold to the
furniture manufacturer as well as the furniture itself. If we
did add both, we would be *double-counting* the wood—when
it was sold to the manufacturer and then again as part of the
finished furniture. We include only the value of the furniture, because the products we are interested in computing
are those made for us to enjoy in the form of finished goods.

Since imported cars and wines are not part of our own nation's product, even though we enjoy them, we should not
include them in the GNP. Imports are part of somebody
else's production. On the other hand, goods we do produce
but which are sent abroad as exports are part of the nation's
product and are included in the GNP.

Clearly, illegal goods and services, such as narcotics, pros-
titution, and so on, are not included. Nor are legal goods and
services that do not enter the market to get a price, such as
work done in the house or garden by the wife or husband. If
a housekeeper or cleaning person has been hired to do the
housework, or a gardener has been employed to work in the
garden, the value of their services (which we measure by
adding their incomes) would be included in the GNP. For
this reason, a man who marries his housekeeper will, if the
number of *household* services remains the same, lower the
GNP. In fact, any services that are not paid for in the market
will be missing from the GNP, even when they should real-

ly be included. For instance, if a piano teacher gives a plumber twenty one-hour lessons in return for unclogging his or her sink, the value of neither the lessons nor the plumbing services will be included. They would only be included if each paid the other with money and they declared these payments as income to the Internal Revenue Service—a declaration that plumbers and piano teachers would probably rather avoid.

A large group of services that do not have a market price are provided by government. Somewhere between a quarter and a half of most Western economies are made up of government services which must be included in the GNP statistics.

How are government services included in the GNP?

Only an absolute cynic or an anarchist would argue that the government produces nothing. Almost everybody else will attach some value to national defense, protection from the evil deeds of fellow citizens, government-sponsored teaching and research, record keeping, memo production, and so on. But how does this value get included in the GNP?

Because little of the government's output is sold directly to the public, we cannot value it as we do the output in the private sector. What we do instead is to value the government's input of human effort that does have a value in the market—the wages and salaries that are paid at every level of government. This means that *all* government salaries are included, whatever is done by the government employee in his civil service. A $50,000 salary for manufacturing red tape or developing better ways of passing bucks gets valued the same as the $50,000 paid for the services of a valuable economist. An obvious question is then:

Are increases in the GNP a good thing?

If a person falls and breaks his arm, the payment to the doctor for repairing the arm is part of the GNP. It follows then that the more people who break their arms, the higher the GNP. Yet, we usually think of higher GNP as a good thing. If an oil tanker were to run aground on the East Coast and the clean-up involved paying thousands of people to work all day and night for days and days to control the spill, the GNP would again rise. But we would not recommend that oil-tanker captains run their ships aground to raise the GNP. Clearly, there are faults in the measure—or at least in the way we use the measure. It is, however, difficult to do much better. Suffice it to say that gross national product is an imperfect measure of the value of goods and services produced by the nation in a year, even if some of the "goods" are "bads."

Are national income and gross national product the same thing?

Yes, essentially they are. Gross national income, frequently referred to simply as national income, is the value of all incomes received by everybody in the nation. Since firms have to pay people for all the producing they do for the firm, and what's left over is profit for the firm and hence part of *its* income, if we added what the firm paid out to people, and its profit, the total would equal the value of its production. Of course, some money must be kept by the firm to replace worn out machinery, and this must be subtracted from production (GNP) to find incomes paid out (national income). Also, certain taxes should not be included in the value of goods produced. But we can almost always use the terms national income and GNP interchangeably.

Are gross national product and gross national expenditures the same?

Again, the answer is yes. We can add the value of all goods and services produced and call it GNP. But since what is produced in generally sold to somebody, we get the same figure by adding up all the expenditures in the nation, which in some countries, including Canada, is called the gross national expenditures, and in the United States is called final sales. If a product is made but not sold, it must have been added to stocks held—that is, inventory—and we must be careful to include this as spending by the firm that added inventory to its stocks. So we see that gross national product, national income, and national expenditures are all different ways of describing the same thing. We might want to use national product when talking about production and national income when talking about income; but since they are more or less equal, don't be confused by thinking these terms have different meanings.

A concept appearing in the GNP statistics that *is* very different is the *real* GNP. In some ways, this is the most important economic statistic.

What is real national product or real GNP?

As soon as the word real is attached to national product or national income we change the meaning in a subtle yet extremely important way. Indeed, what really matters for a nation is its real gross national product. Another expression for real national product is *constant-dollar product.* This gives a better idea of what real magnitudes are about.

The real, or constant dollar, GNP is what the national product would be if prices had never changed. Now, as we are only too aware, prices do change. To get real, or constant-dollar, income, we value the physical amounts that are produced each and every year in terms of prices from some chosen year in the past. We then continue using these same prices in all future years. For example, we might calculate the outputs of all the different items and their prices in 1972—the base currently being used in computing the real GNP. We may then take the outputs of these same items in 1973, 1974, 1975, 1976, and so on and value the output in these years at *1972* prices. Then we compare the GNP from year to year and see how much of a change has taken place in the nation's production. Since the prices we use each time are the same, any change must be because more or less is being produced. And since it is the number of loaves of bread, automobiles, and new houses that really matters for our enjoyment levels, this real GNP concept is very valuable and is much used by the economist. When you hear *growth rates* of the economy, the economist is almost certainly referring to *real,* or *constant*-dollar, GNP. If he isn't and he is talking instead about growth in current-dollar terms, believing what he says to be meaningful, he's probably a poorer economist than you have become by reading this far.

What other adjustments are made to the GNP?

There is one sense in which even real GNP growth doesn't go far enough in describing how much better or worse off we really happen to be. If real GNP is growing only as fast as the number of mouths to feed, bodies to clothe and transport, keep healthy, and so on, then each of us is not better off. To measure our well-being, we would like to know how much real, or constant-dollar, GNP is available for each of us to enjoy. To do this, we divide the real GNP by the population. This is useful in comparing years, and we call the changes between years the *per capita growth rate in real GNP*.

The concept of GNP is even more problematic when comparing the standard of living between countries, even when it is in per capita real terms. High per capita incomes can exist even though only a handful of people are receiving almost the entire amount, so that we wouldn't necessarily call high per capita GNP countries rich or happy ones.

What about seasonal adjustment?

Although the GNP gives the national product for the calendar year, the data are collected each quarter and multiplied by 4 to put them on an annual basis. The quarterly estimates must be seasonally adjusted. This is the only other adjustment made to GNP besides making it real and per capita. It is a fact of life that economic activity regularly picks up at certain times of the year. We wouldn't want to say, for example, "things are getting better" merely because the GNP picked up 1 percent in the third quarter, when the GNP quite regularly rises 2 percent due to the extra summer activity in that quarter. If 2 percent were normal, a 1 percent increase would be a poor performance. To take care of the usual change due to the season, the adjusted figures remove regular seasonal changes. Only if the GNP rises by more than the seasonally normal level based on average patterns over a large number of years will the *seasonally adjusted* GNP be said to have risen.

Seasonal adjustments are made for most economic variables. They can explain why there are more people unemployed in January when there is a decline in the seasonally adjusted unemployment rate. This would happen when the *additional* number of the unemployed is less than usual for that cold month. Of course, the fact that seasonally adjusted unemployment has gone down is cold comfort for those unfortunate people who find themselves unemployed. They might well feel that the government accountant lives on a different planet or is a specialist in some unfathomable magic. It's not unlike the weatherman who calls a northern January night with temperatures a shade above zero a "mild" night. He is adjusting his view to what's seasonally normal. But no matter what he says, it doesn't make it warm.

What are actual values of nominal GNP, real GNP, and so on?

In 1980 the *nominal,* or *current*-dollar, GNP of the United States was approximately $2.62 trillion. Written in full that's $2,620,000,000,000. In 1972 the nominal GNP was rather less than half that amount, at only $1.17 trillion. The nominal GNP rose by such a large amount not because of greater output in 1980 than in 1972, but because of higher prices. The price index for the total GNP, which is equal to 1.0 in the year 1972, had reached the level of 1.80 by 1980. It follows that 80 percent the increase in the nominal, or current-dollar, GNP was due to inflation, at an average compounded rate of 7.6 percent per annum. The value of the *real*, or *constant*-dollar, GNP for 1980 *in terms of the prices of 1972*, was $1.45 trillion. This is $2.62 trillion, divided by the price level of 1.80 for 1980. This compares to the GNP in 1972, when the price index was based at 1.0 of $1.17 trillion. This is a *real* GNP growth from 1972 to 1980 of only 24 percent, which is merely 2.8 percent a year.

The population of the United States in 1972 was 208.8 million. With a GNP in 1972 of $1.17 trillion, that's $5,600 per annum per American. The population of the United States in 1980 was 224.0 million. With a nominal, or current-dollar, GNP of $2.62 trillion, that's $11,700 per annum per American. However, corrected for the 80 percent increase in the price level since 1972, this $11,700 converts into only $6,500 in equivalent 1972 prices. That's a per capita real GNP growth from 1972 to 1980 of about 16 percent, which is below 2 percent a year.

3

MAKING MONEY

The government is the only organization that can operate on a deficit and still make money.

Anonymous

What is money?

Surely, money is the thing for which we work and the thing it is always better to have more of. Wouldn't it surprise you to hear that you're wrong on both counts? Well, you are. Money *isn't* what we earn, and we *can* have too much of it. The trouble is that very many people, including a lot of economists, use the word *money* far too loosely.

Money is what we use to make payments. It is what we use to pay for the groceries, the mortgage, or our taxes. Most immediately, that brings to mind those green pieces of paper— or more colorful ones outside the U.S.—that are invariably decorated with pictures of political or military heroes or living royalty. This, though, is a far too narrow notion of what we use to make payments. The paper bills of the land should strictly be called *currency*, and currency and coins together account for only a small fraction of the total amount of payments that are made in almost any nation. By far the largest fraction of payments are made by giving banks the authority to transfer amounts from the account of one person or company to that of another. The authority is usually in the form of a check that instructs the bank to pay the person or company (or government) the stated amount. Since we have said that money is the thing we use for making payments, this means that the nation's money supply is the total of currency (notes and coins) *plus* the total value of all checkable accounts. This is indeed what we often think of as the money supply—that is, currency plus checkable (or demand) deposits of all banks.

But this concept of money is too narrow. Today it can be a very simple or even automatic process to transfer funds from a savings to a checking account within a bank. Because of such deposit transfers and the newer type of bank accounts that allow payments out of savings accounts, we need to go beyond the narrow notion of a money supply as currency and ordinary checking accounts (M1A) and include those accounts that pay interest, called NOW accounts, and those that allow automatic transfer privileges from savings accounts. We must also include checking accounts outside of the regular commercial banks at the savings and loan associations and credit unions. When these are all put together, we have another concept of the money supply, M1B. But even though this includes most of what can be used in making transactions, it doesn't include everything in the banks.

A more inclusive measure of money is called M2. This adds to the M1B money supply those items that can be quickly converted into a checkable account; it includes the money-market mutual funds, which can be quickly sold, savings or time accounts, and some small items. Since some economists feel the need to go to an even more inclusive definition of the money supply, even more figures are given. Mostly, however, we hear about the M1A, M1B, and M2 money supplies.

Why isn't what we earn money?

It is true that we are paid in the form of money, most commonly by check or perhaps in currency and coins. But what you *earn* is your *income*. This is a very important distinction. Rather than ask you, "How much money do you earn?" I should really say, "What is your income?" I could also ask, "How much money do you own?" You could then add the amount of currency in your purse or wallet to the amount on deposit at the bank and say, "I own such and such a number of dollars." But this would *not* be your income. Your income is so many dollars per month or per week or per year, while the amount of money you have—whatever definition is used—is so many dollars, period. The period of time is irrelevant in figuring out the amount of money you hold, while the income you earn must be expressed as *dollars per period of time*. The same amount of dollars earned within a week is much better than if it takes a whole month. It should now be clear that we work because we want the *income* that is *paid to us in money*. The distinction is crucial. We shall see, for example, that inflation occurs because a nation has too much money flying around. Yes, we can have too much money. It is unlikely that we shall feel that the nation has too much income, especially real income.

Can a person, as well as a country, have too much money?

Again, the answer is yes. Now that we know what we mean by money, we can show why a person can have too much of it. To keep the example straightforward let us think of a person's M1A—namely, his or her currency plus checking deposits in the bank—and imagine that real interest rates on completely safe savings bonds are just 5 percent. How do you think this person would feel about the money in his or her wallet and checking account, which pays no interest, when interest rates on the safe bonds rise to, say, 10 percent per year? Every dollar in the wallet and checking account, when bonds pay 10 percent, means giving up, in lost opportunity, ten cents each year. The economist calls this ten cents the *opportunity cost* per dollar held. You can suspect that some people will want to reduce their holding of money and move it into bonds—which are not themselves money—when interest rates rise. The previously held amount of money will be considered as "too much."

Why, then, do we hold any money at all?

It is true that we lose earning potential if we keep money in our wallets or checking accounts rather than investing it in bonds. But could we keep all of our wealth in forms that pay interest or dividends? Well, it's very difficult to buy a hamburger with a government savings bond. It's equally hard to pay for a new sweater or the dentist's bill in this way. It would also be very inconvenient to cash a bond every time we wanted to buy some groceries. Money in our wallets and checking accounts is very convenient, and that's why money is held. But we pay for the convenience in foregone earnings, which the interest we could receive would otherwise provide.

What types of monies are the most convenient? To answer this, we must ask:

What qualities must money have?

Many different types of monies have existed in the past to help avoid barter—the direct exchange of one product or service for another—with the most commonly used monies consisting of gold or silver. Whatever serves as a medium of exchange must have certain qualities. Clearly, since money is used to store part of our wealth, it must be durable. But this isn't enough. Money must frequently be moved when making payments, so it should be portable. This requires high value for a small volume of whatever we choose, or else it will be too inconvenient. To avoid having people trying to counterfeit what we use as money, the medium should be readily recognizable and difficult to copy, or else have intrinsic value so that it doesn't pay to make copies. It should also be of a standard quality in order to compare one amount with another and be useful as an accounting unit. Furthermore, so that we can use it for a bushel of wheat or an entire wheat farm, it must be easily divisible and capable of being broken down into small amounts or put together in large amounts. With these various requirements, we define money to include currency and deposits in commercial banks and in *near banks,* like credit unions and savings and loan associations. It is clear why. But is this all? For example:

Are credit cards also money?

As things stand, credit cards are *not* included in the money supply. It is not clear whether or not they *should be* included, and economists have only recently begun to tackle the problem. Credit cards are clearly like money in that they can be used to make many different kinds of payments. Unfortunately, though, at some later date we must pay the credit card company the amount we have spent. What the credit card companies do for us is what the name implies—they give us credit. We don't have to pay until they send us the bill at the end of the month, or perhaps a little longer if we are prepared to pay the price. So credit cards are credit. Whether they are also money is not so clear and depends on how people view their cards. About all we can definitely say is that they help us economize on alternative types of money—namely, currency and checks. One check, which requires money in our account only at the end of the month, will suffice for a month of continuous spending.

Money has an effect on the economy when its supply is changed. We should therefore ask how the money supply is changed and in particular:

How can the money supply be increased?

We often talk as if the money supply is increased simply by printing more money. But money, as we have seen, is currency plus bank deposits, and the printed paper with the pictures of old or new celebrities is just the currency component of the overall money supply. The biggest changes in the money supply occur in the very much larger component—the bank deposits. We must therefore see how banks make money. While we will do this for the United States, our account will be accurate for many different countries, where you substitute the name of the appropriate central bank, such as the Bank of Canada, the Bank of England, and so on, for the "Fed."

Who controls the supply of money in the United States?

The United States money supply is controlled by the Federal Reserve System. The U.S. Federal Reserve System consists of a board of governors, with its chairman, centered in Washington, D.C., and twelve district banks. If you check any U.S. bank notes in your wallet or pocketbook, you will find the name of the district bank that issued them. It's written around a circle that is located left of center on the note. You will also notice, at the top, that they are Federal Reserve notes. The twelve United States Federal Reserve banks are in New York, Boston, Chicago, Cleveland, Philadelphia, Richmond, St. Louis, Atlanta, Kansas City, Dallas, Minneapolis, and San Francisco. The entire Federal Reserve System collectively constitutes the United States' equivalent of other countries' central banks.

In the United States, a number of the larger private or commercial banks maintain deposits with their local Federal Reserve bank. This is the leading component of the commercial banks' "reserve." The remainder of their reserves is currency in their vaults. The commercial banks must ensure that their total reserves—deposits with the Fed plus the currency that they hold—are always kept above a required fraction of the value of their customers' deposits. This fraction is called the *minimum reserve ratio*.

It is wasteful for the commercial banks to hold much in the way of excess reserves, and they therefore usually have as large a volume of customer deposits as these reserves will allow. As a consequence, the amount of deposits that people have with the commercial banks—which is a large part of the money supply—can be increased only if the banks' reserves are increased.

How does the Fed change the banks' reserves?

If the Fed wishes to change the supply of money, its first and most usual line of action is to use *open-market operations*. This means the buying or selling of treasury bills or bonds on the open market—the market that is open to a very wide range of traders who, in the United States, live primarily in New York City. A desired increase in reserves—and therefore in the money supply—requires that the Fed purchase treasury bills or bonds in this open market. The treasury bills are originally sold by the Department of the Treasury but it is only if the bills are purchased by the Fed, either when issued or later, that the money supply is increased. The money supply increase occurs because in buying treasury bills, the Fed writes checks against itself that eventually become commercial bank reserves.

If the sellers of the bills or bonds to the Fed are commercial banks, the payment from the Federal Reserve bank means a direct increase in the commercial banks' deposits with the Fed—that is, the commercial banks' reserves. The same outcome will occur if the seller of the bills or bonds is not a commercial bank, but it will occur indirectly. When the seller takes the check received from the Fed to his commercial bank, the commercial bank will present the Fed's check to the Fed itself. The Fed will credit the commercial bank's account, which results in an increase in the bank's reserves.

What do extra reserves mean?

With more reserves, the banks will be able to create more deposits and still maintain the required ratio of reserves to deposits—more reserves allow more bank deposits. Commercial banks can increase deposits by the public if they make more loans to the public. A bank loan simply means that the bank raises its balance in your account, and you sign the obligation to repay the bank, with interest. And since bank deposits are a leading component of the money supply, we find that more reserves which result from open-market purchases, will allow the commercial banks to offer more loans and thereby create a bigger supply of money. Just as open-market *purchases* will allow banks to raise the supply of money, so, in the opposite manner, do open-market *sales* force the banks to lower the supply of money because it reduces their reserves and hence their ability to offer loans.

How else is the supply of money changed?

There are a couple of less often used procedures for changing the money supply. One way is to reduce the fraction of total value of deposits that the commercial bank must maintain on reserve with the district Federal Reserve bank. If the required fraction drops, the same reserves allow more deposits to be created through granting loans—that is, increasing the money supply. Alternatively, the Fed or central bank could allow the banks to borrow from them and thereby raise the size of their reserves on account with the Fed or central bank. The Fed or central bank can encourage or discourage this commercial bank borrowing by changing the rate of interest it charges—the *discount rate.* In some countries without well-developed money and capital markets, changes in reserve requirements or in discount rates are more often used than in the United States. But although these same alternatives exist in the United States, Canada, and Great Britain, the most frequently used procedure for changing the money supply, because these countries have well-developed markets, is open-market operations. And we will soon see the powerful effect the money supply can have, especially in fueling inflation.

Something that is frequently described as inflationary is a situation where the government spends more than it receives. But does this increase the supply of money?

Is the money supply raised when the government spends more than it receives?

In practice, when the government spends more than it receives, this does tend to mean more money in circulation. But this need not be so.

The government—or, more precisely, the Treasury, which is the taxing and spending branch of the government—can finance its excess of spending over receipts by selling its treasury bills or bonds in the open market and then using the proceeds to cover its budgetary gap. If the funds are raised from the sale of bills or bonds to the public, then the money supply remains unchanged when the proceeds are spent by the Treasury. All that happens is that the government spends the money, rather than someone in the private sector. For example, if the government spends $10 billion more than it receives in taxes by selling $10 billion of bonds to the public, that is $10 billion of money taken from private hands. At this point, the money supply has been reduced by $10 billion. But when the government spends the $10 billion, it goes right back into circulation. An open-market sale of treasury bills or bonds to the public therefore changes only *who* spends the money. It does not itself add to the supply of money.

The money supply grows when, instead of selling bonds to the public, the Treasury sells them to the central bank—the Federal Reserve System. The Federal Reserve will "pay" for the bonds by crediting the Treasury's account with them, $10 billion in our example. The government's account at the Fed is not itself money, but when the Treasury spends the proceeds of its bond sale, it will write $10 billion of checks against its deposits at the Fed. This, then, works just like an open-market purchase of bonds. When the commercial banks receive and return the checks that the Treasury drew against its account at the Fed, the banks will be credited with them. But the deposits at the Fed are the reserves of the commercial banks. More reserves mean more commercial bank loans can take place, which means a growth in the money supply.

Thus, if the government finances its excess of spending over receipts by selling bonds to the public, there should not be an increase in the money supply. If, however, the bonds are sold to the Fed, commercial bank reserves will grow as the proceeds are spent, and so will the nation's money supply.

With the banking system of the United States so well developed, it is difficult to believe that it is so new. But open-market operations, the Fed, and even its currency, did not exist until the twentieth century.

What is the history of money?

Money didn't get invented overnight. It developed and evolved over centuries. Indeed, long ago, paper money wouldn't have been worth the paper it was printed on. You might well believe that we are fast approaching that point again. But the reason for the problem long ago was not that there was too much paper money—rather, it was because it just didn't exist at all.

In days long gone, the inconvenience of barter gave way to the use of a commodity money like gold. Gold is easily divisible, nonperishable, easily portable, and generally recognizable. And so the world flourished or floundered with payments made in various amounts of gold. Perhaps even more than today, there was no shortage of people in those times who would have been happy to relieve you of the burden of your wealth. And without the help of well-developed insurance schemes, theft was a risk few could hardly afford. Therefore, as people held gold while they looked for things to buy, they needed a secure place to keep it in.

Where did people keep gold?

Before there were banks, as we know them today, few people had safes in which to keep their valued things. Goldsmiths, however, whose occupation made it necessary to work with gold and precious stones, did own safes. People who owned lots of gold would ask their local goldsmith if he would help take care of it and, for a small fee, he might oblige.

By its very nature, money is not consumed and is not in use all the time. The goldsmiths, if they had not known of this before, soon found it out, simply by noticing how long it would lie idle in their vaults. They learned that they could turn these idle funds to very good use.

It was not uncommon for people whom the goldsmiths could trust to come into their shops and ask for a loan. With all that stuff just sitting in the vault, and people not coming back for it for long periods of time, why not loan a little out—at an interest rate, of course? Since only a limited number of the people who had entrusted their bullion to the goldsmiths were likely to turn up on any particular day to retrieve it, the goldsmiths could have quite a bit out on loan and still meet the daily demands.

What added to the goldsmiths' ability to make interest-earning loans was the fact that some of the depositors hardly ever came back at all. The goldsmiths, to keep track of what had been left in their care, issued paper receipts that might read, "The holder of this receipt has entrusted and stored with me one ounce of fine gold." And if the holder of such a note made a purchase from another that required payment of an ounce of gold, he might easily pay his obligation with his note. Indeed, to make it even easier for their customers to pay, the goldsmiths might issue many pieces of paper, each for a small part of what had been taken on deposit. And so paper money was born.

When did fractional reserves begin?

The goldsmiths' business of granting loans became so profitable that many of them gave up the jewelry trade. By issuing notes against what they held in reserve, they could earn a steady interest. They eventually began to issue more paper than they had gold, because the paper would merely keep on circulating and not too many came in to redeem their gold at any one time. This is the fractional-reserve banking system.

However, there was a limit on the volume of paper the goldsmiths could loan because of the limit on the size of their reserves. Prudence dictated that not so much paper should circulate that they might occasionally get caught short. The more gold they held, the more money they could loan by printing up paper. And the more paper they loaned, the more interest it allowed them to earn.

And so the goldsmiths competed with each other for the deposit of gold, each reducing his fee and even by offering interest to those who deposited with him. Thus we had the system of private banks, with their own notes in circulation and with gold held on account. Things didn't remain private for long. The government soon became involved.

Why did government get involved?

Very few profitable enterprises can long escape the watchful and hungry eye of government. As the profit opportunities became obvious, virtually every national government, including that of the United States, took over the right to print up the money receipts and hold its own reserve of gold. Eventually, as the money was made *legal tender*, it was even possible to remove the promise to redeem it in gold. The money became *fiat*, not because of the name of the car, but to signify that it contained no value in terms of metal.

Even with silver coins, the government can get a take. By adding base metals to silver coins, it can stretch more out of a limited amount of silver, but it can still stamp them as "one dollar" and spend them as such. The profit from thus debasing the coin has become known as *seigniorage*.

What was the result of having both debased and good money in circulation?

There's an interesting rule that relates to the circulation of debased coins next to the real thing. If you are to make payment for something and you hold both silver coins and those containing base metal, you won't use the silver ones, and so the good money does not circulate. This is known as Gresham's law, the fact that "bad money drives out good."

What has happened this century?

Commercial banks have been established with legally mandated fractional-reserve rules. What they must hold as required reserves are currency and deposits at the Federal Reserve, which was set up in 1913. The Federal Reserve used to maintain a minimum ratio of gold to back up the money that exists, but when the gold flowed out and the money supply expanded in the 1960s, that backing was removed. They still hold some gold, but it has no prescribed bearing on the supply of money. More or less gold nowadays means very little at all, unless you happen to own it yourself.

That brings us to today. Will banking remain like this?

What is the future of money?

Money has moved into the electronic age. It is not too difficult to see how far this can go.

Imagine that each seller is hooked into a giant computer,

which also processes all payments and receipts. This computer inputs your income and maintains your bank account. As you make any purchase—large or small—you give an identification card or code, and the seller enters the amount into his console. The giant computer, almost as quickly as the signal can pass along the wire, credits the seller's account and debits or reduces your own. There's no need to write a check or even pay a charge account bill at the end of the month.

The computer or computers that would be required to handle the electronic payments system in this way would have to be massive. But there are other problems that have to be faced. For example, how do you ensure that your account does not contain a mistake, and how do you discover and prove where it is when it does? How do you keep people from "plugging in" just to find out how much money you have? And what about tracing your movements and activities by seeing what transactions you have made? And how do you pay the fare for a bus or cab?

There are many problems to be solved in a full-fledged "electronic funds transfer system," or EFTS, and some monies in the old form are likely to survive. But we can be assured that the evolution of the monetary system is not yet complete.

Now we are ready to explain inflation and unemployment. We will show how inflation is fueled by increasing the growth rate of the money supply and how unemployment is caused by the reverse—a reduction in the growth rate of the money supply.

4

WHAT CAUSES
INFLATION AND
UNEMPLOYMENT?

I don't think the President understands why there's high inflation and high unemployment at the same time. But then neither does anybody else.

Unnamed Treasury official

Does anyone have the answers?

If economists really know what causes inflation and unemployment, why don't we hire them to get rid of both problems? The answer to this second question gives us the answer to the first. Since we all know that inflation and unemployment are bad things and we would like to eliminate them, the fact that these problems exist and persist is evidence in itself that we do not know how to get rid of them. We do not know how to get rid of them because there's no consensus on the cause. But this doesn't mean that every economist doesn't *think* he has all the answers. The problem is that they all disagree. It is important to remember this when you find yourself involved in a discussion about economics at a cocktail party and feel reluctant to venture an opinion. It is absolutely safe to disagree with what everybody else is saying. Indeed, if you do not disagree, people will become suspicious about what you know. It is in the nature of economists to disagree. On the factors that lie behind inflation and unemployment there is complete disagreement. Whatever you say will be in agreement with some and in disagreement with others, so say it forcefully.

Within the many different views of what causes inflation and unemployment, there are two leading schools, or camps—the monetarists and the Keynesians—the latter named after the late British economist, Lord John Maynard Keynes. Virtually every economist is branded according to which of these schools he or she follows. Explaining what it means to be a monetarist or a Keynesian involves giving their views on what causes inflation and unemployment and how to cure them. While their differences are substantial, they do tend to exaggerate them just to stay loyal to their respective camps. Let's start with the monetarists and their view of the cause of inflation.

THE MONETARISTS

What does a monetarist view as the cause of inflation?

Monetarists argue that inflation is caused by too much money (which we recall is currency plus certain bank deposits) chasing after too few goods. This explanation or theory is given the name of the *quantity theory of money.*

What is the quantity theory of money?

Imagine a land with a marvelous type of tree. The fruit of this tree has the miraculous property of being edible, wearable, and combustible for heat and light. All the needs in the land are met by this fruit. It should come as no surprise to learn that this tree is in short supply, that only one thousand pieces of fruit grow from the trees in any given year, and that all the trees are owned by the same company, which sells all the fruit to the people who need them. Imagine that in this land there are one thousand pieces of green paper issued by the government on which it is written, "This note is legal tender," and on which there is a picture of a man with white hair. These are one-dollar bills.

Now, if each piece of paper were used once during the year, the total amount of money to change hands would be one thousand dollars. With one thousand dollars changing hands during the year in exchange for the one thousand pieces of fruit, what was the average price for each fruit? The answer is clearly an average of one dollar each.

Let us now suppose that the government decides to print up another one thousand pieces of the same green paper and that all two thousand pieces continue to change hands once a year, just like the first thousand pieces did. The speed, or velocity, of circulation of the money is, in other words, unchanged. With one thousand pieces of fruit going one way and the two thousand dollars changing hands the other way, the fruit must cost an average of two dollars each.

With two thousand pieces of paper changing hands at a once-a-year rate, only if the number of fruits were to grow to twice as many, that is, two thousand a year, would their prices remain at one dollar each. We see that when the increase in the number of pieces of paper is greater than the growth in the number of goods, prices will rise. That's why it can be said that inflation arises from too much money chasing too few goods. Inflation results from increasing the money supply at too fast a rate, at least to a monetarist.

You might be thinking at this point: "But what if, when you doubled the number of pieces of paper, they started to change hands only once every two years?" In other words, what happens if the speed, or velocity, of circulation halves when the money supply is doubled? Then, with two thousand pieces of paper in existence, but only one thousand changing hands in the year, there would be one thousand dollars' worth of transactions each year. With one thousand pieces of fruit changing hands, this fruit will still cost an average of a dollar a piece. This now becomes an important question. Does the speed, or velocity, with which money changes hands fall at the same rate as the money supply is increased? The answer is that numerous studies over many years and in different countries show that this hasn't happened. The velocity of circulation of money has been relatively stable. That's why more money means higher prices. And that's the quantity theory of money. The bigger the quantity of money, the higher prices become.

Why, then, would the government want to issue extra paper?

Now we are getting down to the juicy and prime question. The extra paper that the government prints could be used by the government to buy goods and services for itself. Indeed, that's the way to get the money into circulation. The government can use the money it prints to make purchases. This saves the government from having to explicitly tax people to get the funds to buy the same items. In other words, the government will want to issue extra paper when the people would object to paying extra taxes.

Does the printing of money constitute a tax?

Simply stated, yes. It is a hidden tax. Through printing money, the government can get a bigger share of the national pie. There are no visible deductions from paychecks, so, in effect, the government gets its slice through the back door without people realizing it. This immediately begs the question:

Who does pay the tax from printing money?

Well, clearly someone paid or the government would not have gotten its goods. But nobody had anything deducted, so who paid the tax? The answer is that it is the holders of money who pay the tax on the government issuing new money. We can see this in terms of our previous example.

Before there was more money printed, there were one thousand "one-dollar" units of paper money. With prices at one dollar per fruit, these one thousand bills bought one thousand fruits. After the government prints an extra thousand pieces of paper, we now know that prices go up to two dollars per fruit. What happens now to the people who hold the original one thousand dollar bills? Well, now, at two dollars per fruit, they will be able to buy only five hundred fruits. Who gets the rest? The government gets the other five hundred with its newly printed money. Thus, it is the holders of the old bills who pay the tax—five hundred fruits worth.

Can we see the inflation tax in a different way?

We can see the hidden tax of inflation in an entertaining way by tackling an extremely clever Ph.D. exam question that was asked at the University of Chicago. The question goes like this:

"There once was an upright and very proper Englishman who regularly took his summer vacation on a tiny, agreeable, Aegean island. The Englishman had returned to the island so many times that his credit worthiness had been established beyond any possible doubt. There was absolutely no chance that this Englishman's bank would fail to honor his checks and, indeed, all of them had always been honored promptly.

"Since the Englishman's credit was so sound, the islanders were totally happy to allow him to pay by check, with the certain knowledge that they were good checks. Indeed, so well known and trusted was the Englishman on this tiny island that the islanders were happy to accept the Englishman's checks from each other. For example, if the restaurateur wished to pay the grocer partly with a check he had received in payment for a meal, the grocer was happy to accept the check. The grocer was then able to buy gas with the check, and the Englishman's checks circulated in this way around the island. Indeed, the checks were never returned to the Englishman's London bank for collection."

The University of Chicago exam question then read: "Who paid for the Englishman's holiday?" Well, who did?

Who paid for the holiday?

Clearly, the Englishman did not pay, since the checks were never returned to London. Then it was obviously the islanders, but which one of them? Because there is no last person to hold the checks—since everyone can spend the checks and everyone will accept them—it is not the last people holding the checks. O.K., then, who?

The answer is that all the islanders paid, and not just the ones who sold things to the Englishman. They all paid because their willingness to accept the Englishman's checks had put the Englishman in the position of being able to "print" money. He had become like the central bank in every country, which can print money that people are willing to hold. (Indeed, they must hold central bank money since it is legal tender. It is against the law not to accept it.) By "printing" money, the Englishman had raised the tiny island's money supply. And as we know from the quantity theory of money, if we print more money, we raise prices. How, then, had the islanders paid for the holiday? They paid by being left with reduced buying power because of the higher prices. They paid through the inflation brought about by the circulation of the checks.

Where do the goods and services come from?

The goods and services consumed by the Englishman with his newly created "money"—given an unchanged output of goods and services on the island—leaves fewer goods and services for the islanders to enjoy. Since governments throughout the world have the right to print money, when they do this they have the same effect as the Englishman's "printing" money during his summer vacations. By printing money, the government becomes able to enjoy a fraction of the goods and services that the nation can produce without having to pay for them. It does not pay in the sense that the money it prints costs no more than the price of the paper and ink used, which is probably a fraction of a cent. But by writing "one dollar" on the note, the government can enjoy a dollar's worth of goods and services. And if it's profitable to print a one-dollar bill, it must be fantastically more profitable to print a one-hundred-dollar bill. All that is needed is a different arrangement of ink with a couple of zeros and a different ex-president. Even ledger entries will do. Yet these cheap-to-produce bits of money give the government the opportunity to enjoy a vast volume of goods and services. It can buy lunches, plane rides to foreign trade meetings and faraway lands, jets, bombs, typewriters, income-tax forms, secretarial help, and a whole lot more.

Now, the government can also buy all the things it wants by taxing us explicitly with income and corporate taxes. But it gets the same thing through printing money, which is, in every way, as much of a tax; it increases the share of the pie going to the government. We pay this tax through inflation. As with the Englishman on the island, the inflation that results from printing money reduces the value of the preexisting money. The goods and services that the money would have bought before the inflation are the goods and services enjoyed by the government with its hidden tax. The government can do this because few people recognize that the printing of money, and the resulting inflation, is a tax. The more of us who are alerted to this, the more likely it is to stop.

But what is the effect of *decreasing* the money supply? A revealing way of understanding this is to look at the effect of destroying money.

What is the effect of burning dollar bills?

We are told, by people who wish to reveal the crudeness of those who made great profits in America's past, of extravagant dinner parties with overweight robber barons lighting their cigars with one-hundred-dollar bills. (Well, perhaps they were ten-dollar bills, but why be cheap in our account?) What a terrible waste this must seem with so many millions starving. You might be very surprised to hear that, in reality, there was no waste in this activity at all. Indeed, these robber barons were being very generous.

What was destroyed in the demonstration of great affluence was a piece of paper, nothing more. This meant, of course, that the capitalist who burned the money couldn't go out and enjoy what the $100 would buy. But what happened to the real goods and services that he could have purchased? This is what really matters to society, not the piece of paper. No real goods were destroyed. The barons just gave up the ability to buy the goods. These goods must therefore have become available to others to buy and enjoy. What an unselfish act our American industrial barons performed in reducing the money supply to raise others' buying power. And when Mr. D. B. Cooper jumped off his plane with $200,000 that he never got to spend, he did the rest of us—not those who supplied the money—a good turn. Are you convinced it is done with mirrors? You might also be convinced that we have forgotten other factors, such as oil prices, that lie behind inflation.

Can inflation be explained without looking at individual prices, such as those of oil?

Inflation, as we have said, is the rate of increase in prices in general, and since oil is an important commodity, we would expect an increase in inflation to occur as its price rises at a faster rate. Indeed, since oil is both bought directly, to heat homes and fuel automobiles, and indirectly, in the transportation of almost everything we buy and the production of many things, oil price increases should be inflationary. At least this seems reasonable. So, wouldn't it surprise you to know that increases in the price of oil do not themselves substantially contribute to inflation? You are surely shocked at that statement, so let us see why.

We are all aware of the limits that exist on what we have available to spend. Just as the national income is limited because of scarcity of inputs, so is the individual income of the average citizen limited. If, after taxes and other deductions from a salary or wage check, there is, for example, $2000 to spend, you can choose what to spend it upon. Some income might be required for mortgage payments, savings plans, and such, and only a certain limited amount will remain.

Suppose you are forced to drive your car to get to work and to go to important places, and you are not able to reduce the number of gallons that you must put in the tank. If each fill-up costs $20 and you fill up four times a month, that's $80 out of what is available to spend on other things. Now suppose there is a doubling in the price of gasoline. That's a whopping $160 a month, just to fuel the car. But that will mean $80 less to spend on everything else. There is less available for eating out and new pairs of jeans. Something, somewhere in your expenditures must be reduced, and whatever it is, there are fewer dollars pouring into the pockets of the people who provide these things.

Initially, there is no question but that oil price increases will raise the cost of living. Lots of prices rise, including heating oil and gasoline, and others do not come down. But what happens to all the prices of goods and services that remain unsold because we don't have the available income to buy them? These prices will not decline quickly. But they don't have to. All that is necessary to reduce the inflation in these prices is to have them rise *less quickly*. And that's what will happen if no one buys the items because more money is required to pay for oil and gasoline.

In most countries today, the effect we have described is not likely to run its course and bring down the rate of inflation in items other than oil. Before prices—or even rates of price increases—begin to decline, all the income siphoned off for oil causes unemployment elsewhere. We've witnessed this happen before. And to prevent unemployment from becoming severe, the government prints money and stimulates the economy and thereby "accommodates" the increased oil prices. But it is the creation of money, along the lines of the quantity theory, that causes prices to continually rise, not the price rise in oil itself. And it is even less the result of the price of oil if, by conservation, our consumption of it can decline. This is the monetarist view. Many other economists wouldn't agree.

But if increases in oil prices shouldn't cause continuous inflation, how about rising wages? Can wage demands cause inflation?

Does a monetarist believe that wage increases cannot cause inflation?

It might appear, from what we have been saying, that, to a monetarist, only money matters and wage increases cannot spark and maintain inflation. Yet in discussions of inflation a once highly popular distinction was that between *cost-push* and *demand-pull* varieties of the problem. Cost-push inflation originates through excessive wage increases. Inflation caused by higher wages results when firms increase their prices to offset wage hikes and thus avoid a reduction in profits. Higher prices of the goods that workers buy increases pressure for further wage increases, which leads to further price increases, and so on. On the other hand, the description of demand-pull inflation begins with an increase in the aggregate demand for goods. This then raises prices, which leads to pressure for wage increases, and so on. The only difference between the two explanations of inflation is in the origin of the problem. Cost-push inflation starts with labor—especially if it unionized—and demand-pull inflation begins with aggregate demand.

Clearly, wage increases don't help inflation, but by walking into the boss's office and demanding $200 an hour, you'll soon be making more humble demands elsewhere. The monetarist says that a given amount of money would have to move around very fast to pay everyone $200 or more an hour. However, since the velocity of circulation of money is limited, with a fixed amount of money, wages can't be that high. Wage increases can cause prices to go up, but there is a limit on what can happen before firms are put out of business and workers are forced to moderate their demands. This all follows if the government is smart. But what might happen if it is not?

*What happens if the government accommodates
wage increases?*

A not-too-clever economic authority might help fuel an
inflation that is started by excessive wage demands. If people are not employed because wages are too high, the government might try to create more aggregate demand. This
could involve more money being printed, which could help
maintain higher wages and prices. Wage increases might
again follow price increases, and if the government tries to
keep full employment through increases in aggregate demand, inflation would be an inevitable result. But even
though started by a cost increase, this inflation involves the
government because it helped to create excessive demand.
For this reason, a monetarist considers that an economist is
about as well served in studying cost-and-demand origins of
inflation as in studying the chronological order of the chick-
en and the egg. But, with the monetarist's view of inflation
now explained, what about the monetarist's view of what
causes unemployment?

How do monetarists view unemployment?

First of all, let us remember that full employment exists
even when some people are out of work or are searching for
jobs. We said, in defining full employment, that with shifts
of demand between different products and with people
looking for better opportunities, we would have 5 or even 6
percent unemployment, even when we say that there is full
employment. This sort of unemployment—call it structural
or frictional if you like—is not necessarily unhealthy, and
the cause is merely that we live in a dynamic world that is

experiencing change. So, in asking what causes unemployment, we are really asking what causes unemployment at levels above the healthy 5 or 6 percent level. This leads us to the monetarist explanation of higher unemployment.

The unemployed are people looking for work. If 1 million people, for example, leave their jobs each month—either voluntarily or without choice—and search for new jobs, and if they each take an average of one month before finding their new employment, there will be an average of one million people looking for work at any given time. Now, if the same number—that is, 1 million—leave jobs each month and spend two months looking for work, then at any given time we'll find about two million people unemployed. In other words, given just normal turnover between jobs, the longer people are forced or choose to look before taking new jobs, the higher the rate of unemployment will be. It follows that in providing an explanation for higher unemployment, we must look at *why* people are spending more time finding a job that they can and want to take.

What determines when you will take a job?

We all have in mind an idea of what we are worth, and this sets a floor on what we will accept. If you were a $50,000-a-year company executive, you would be unlikely to accept a $40,000 salary to do essentially the same job. You would be even less likely to accept a job as a bus driver. If you earned $25,000 as a school teacher, you are unlikely to accept a $20,000 teaching job, and even less likely to take a $10-an-hour job as a janitor. A $10-an-hour janitor will not take a $5-an-hour job as a dishwasher, and if the janitor quit his job voluntarily, he will not be apt to take another job if it pays what he was previously earning. It would have to be a better paying job than before—that is, more than $10 an hour—to be acceptable, since the old job was unacceptable at that wage.

Even during relatively slack times, there are job vacancies. If you don't believe this, take a look at employment opportunities in a newspaper or call any employment agency, either public or private. Once we accept this, we can develop an excellent understanding of the cause of unemployment if we remember two things. First, the longer people search before taking a job, the higher the rate of unemployment will be. We established this with our one-month versus two-month illustration. Second, there are always job vacancies, but sometimes there are more vacancies than at other times. The two big theories of unemployment can be derived from these two notions, although each theory puts a different emphasis on the two variables. The monetarists' theory is called the *search theory*.

What is the search theory?

The search-theory of unemployment that is associated with the monetarist school says roughly this: When inflation has been running steadily at, say, 8 percent, with wages rising at, say 10 percent (the 2-percent difference, or real gain, is the result of productivity, which used to grow), there'll be some normal, or *natural*, rate of unemployment. These are the people naturally looking to trade up or drop out or in other ways increase their satisfaction. A person leaving a $10-an-hour job can look for $11 an hour and eventually get it, if only because of inflation. Indeed, people need to get increases just to compensate for the higher prices.

Now, according to this search theory, if inflation begins to fall, say, to 5 percent, wages might grow at only 7 percent.

The person who used to earn $10 an hour and is holding out for $11 an hour will now have to wait longer to find it. And, as we have seen, if they wait and search longer, unemployment is higher. In other words, we have unemployment rising when the rate of inflation *begins to drop*. More precisely, we have unemployment rising when inflation is lower than people anticipated it would be. Of course, with inflation lower than anticipated, a $10.50-an-hour job, for example, will be as good as an $11-an-hour job would have been with the higher inflation that had been anticipated. People will begin to take jobs when they learn about this, but while they are learning, they continue looking and are still unemployed.

Then what makes unemployment decline?

The argument of the search theorists also works in reverse. When inflation picks up from, say, 5 percent to 10 percent, and wage rates start to grow faster, increasing from, say, 7 percent to 12 percent, people will spend less time searching for a new job. A person who earned $10 an hour might be holding out for $10.50 if he had been used to wages that had been growing at 5 percent a year. If, however, the rate at which wages are increasing rises to 12 percent a year, the person will find the $10.50 job he is seeking much more quickly. Someone taking a job more quickly means a lower rate of unemployment. When inflation grows faster than people had anticipated people accept jobs more quickly. As a result, unemployment tends to drop. When people again learn what inflation is doing and anticipate it correctly, they do not accept jobs any more quickly than normal. We then have a normal, or natural, rate of unemployment.

The simple relationship whereby unemployment is lower when inflation is higher, and vice versa, is known as the "Phillips curve" after A. W. Phillips of the London School of Economics and Australian National University. We have just claimed that, to monetarists, unemployment is lower when inflation grows more rapidly than had been anticipated, but this notion has been challenged by those who believe that workers are rational.

What if workers are rational?

Some economists, such as Robert Lucas and Thomas Sargent, have argued that if workers employ every piece of information available about factors affecting inflation, they will make no consistent errors. Then, inflation will only temporarily be more or less than anticipated. If this is true, unemployment will randomly fluctuate about the natural rate. Economic policy that uses inflation to reduce unemployment by having people underestimate inflation will no longer work. The money supply then becomes "neutral" vis-à-vis unemployment, real output, and such.

This rational-expectations view does have a good deal of merit, but there seems little doubt that workers have made consistent errors in forecasting inflation, so that our monetary theory does apply over certain periods of time. But is this the only theory that applies at these times and, if not, is there a theory that applies at all times? Keynesians use the same theory in their explanation of both inflation and unemployment. They believe it always works.

THE KEYNESIANS

What do Keynesians look at?

Keynesians concentrate on the *circular flow of income*. This circular flow is from firms to consumers as wages and then from consumers back to firms as payments for purchases made by consumers. Keynesians view the circular flow from firms to consumers and back again as being consistent with a steady level of prices and employment, as long as the flow itself is steady. However, there are "leakages" and "injections" that affect these flows. Leakages occur because most consumers don't spend everything they earn and because the government takes taxes. Injections occur when business invests—buys extra plant and equipment—and when government spends.

The balance between leakages and injections is what lies behind Keynesian views of both inflation and unemployment. When total injections exceed leakages, they expect inflation, and when the process is reversed, they expect unemployment. As an analogy, they refer to baths and washbasins. When we inject more water into a bath or bowl than the drain can handle, the water level will rise and eventually it will overflow. Similarly, if business invests and government spends—both injections—more than consumers save and government taxes—both leakages—the economy overflows and we have what Keynesians call an *inflationary gap*. This attributes inflation to situations where we attempt to invest more than we save, and where the government spends more than it taxes. When the situation is reversed and injections fall short of leakages, we have a *deflationary gap* that lies behind the Keynesian view of unemployment. Additional leakage occurs when consumers purchase goods from abroad and offsetting injection occurs when we sell exports. This source of inflationary and deflationary gaps is usually ignored. It is, however, very similar to the others.

What does a Keynesian view as causing inflation?

Keynesians view inflation as being the result of injections being greater than leakages *only* after we have reached full employment. When there is lots of slack because of unemployment, they believe that injections by the government (that exceed leakages) will do only good and will create jobs. Only after full employment is reached will an inflationary gap occur. This encourages fine tuning by government and is very different from the quantity-theory conclusion, which explains the gulf between Keynesians and monetarists. Since we have observed over many periods of history and in numerous economies a combination of inflation with unemployment, we know that the mutually exclusive nature of the two in Keynesian theory needs extensive revision.

Keynes wrote about unemployment because that was the main problem at the time when he was writing. His followers have made changes in his theory.

What does a Keynesian view as the cause of unemployment?

We have already answered this when we said that Keynesians view unemployment as the reverse of inflation. They believe unemployment comes from deflationary gaps, where total leakages exceed injections. But this begs the very important question of how total leakages could exceed total injections. This requires either that savings exceed investment or that taxes exceed government spending—or both.

Taxes and government spending are determined by largely political decisions within the government, and we need no clever theories to explain what makes them unequal. However, the difference between savings and investment *does* need some theoretical explanation.

What makes savings exceed investment?

Savings and investment both depend on interest rates. If events reduce the desire of businessmen to invest in new plants and equipment, they do not demand funds that have been saved. The resultant surplus of savings in the financial markets causes the lenders of these funds to reduce the interest rates they are charging. The reduced rates of interest make more businessmen want to borrow because, at low rates, they can find more profitable uses for the funds. And so, even if investment were to initially decline below savings, this would reduce the rate of interest and cause more people to want to borrow and invest.

In addition to the effect of lower interest rates in encouraging extra spending on plant and equipment—that is, investment—there is a reinforcing effect of lower interest rates reducing savings. A case can be made both ways, but it is generally said that lower interest rates reduce the amount that people save. It follows that if investment declines, making savings exceed investment, and then interest rates are reduced, this will not only raise investment but will lower savings. With higher investment and lower savings, the shortage of investment over savings will quickly be eliminated.

If what we have said is true, then what reason can a

Keynesian give for persistent unemployment due to savings exceeding investment? What is it that prevents them from becoming equal?

What makes savings plans differ from investment plans?

Keynes argued that investors base decisions on animal spirit. His rationale went like this: No businessman will be able to tell the value of extra profit from a new machine or other additional piece of capital equipment over the full life of the equipment. Capital investments last for many years. It is not only difficult to tell what profit will be coming from today's investment after another *ten* years, but it is even difficult to say what will happen in the *next* year. Because of future uncertainties, businessmen base their decisions on their feelings for what the future holds in store. If, for some reason, they feel negative, they will not borrow, whatever the interest rate.

But can't the interest rate decline enough so that the advantage of borrowing is so obvious that it will overcome even the animal spirit? Here Keynes had a different answer that depends on the *liquidity trap.*

What is the liquidity trap?

During the early 1930s interest rates on bonds were extremely low—just a couple of percentage points. Keynes argued that if it became generally believed that rates were already so low that they could only rise, the public would not wish to buy bonds. If they did buy them and interest rates did indeed later rise, nobody would buy *their* bonds, with the *new* bonds offering higher interest rates, unless they sold their bonds cheaply. In short, they would lose money on the low interest rate bonds they held and therefore, instead of putting funds in bonds, people held their wealth as ready cash or, at most, in very short-term investments. What is more, if the monetary authority raised the money supply, people merely held the money rather than buying bonds. If savers don't loan newly created money to the investors—the issuers of bonds—unemployment will not be eliminated by creating more money, and we are in a liquidity trap.

Now there are a couple of problems with the argument we have given. For example: "How can people generally think interest rates will rise without them actually rising?" And: "How can the money supply be increased if people don't want to borrow?" The key feature, however, of the Keynesian argument is that if unemployment exists because savings exceed investment, and declines in interest rates cannot eliminate this deflationary gap, then what must be done is to raise government spending or reduce taxes. Those who emphasize monetary policy, on the other hand, say that even if Keynes were right about the situation at the time in which he wrote, the reluctance to buy bonds with newly made money did not exist at other times in recent history. Moreover, they will say that even if investment and savings do give us a deflationary gap, we cannot have persistent unemployment if wages are flexible. Flexible wages allow the unemployed to work for the lower wages that businessmen may be prepared to offer. Keynesians answer this with the proposition that wages are rigid in a downward direction.

What is the role of rigid wages in Keynes's view of unemployment?

Keynes recognized that if unemployment existed, it could be speedily corrected *if* the unemployed, and others, were prepared to accept lower wages than those that had previously prevailed. Unemployment simply means that the supply of labor exceeds the demand for it. If the excess of supply brought down the price, or the wage, to the point where demand equals supply, then there would be no unemployment. The persistence of unemployment, which Keynes thought could be corrected only through fiscal-demand creation from increasing government spending or from reducing taxes, could result only from a downward rigidity of wages. Keynes argued that such downward rigidity in wages does exist.

The debate can be taken further by distinguishing between the buying power of wages—that is, real wages—and the simple dollar wage. The real wage can be reduced by inflation—at least for a while—and inflation resulting from printing more money can therefore temporarily stimulate lower unemployment.

Is this a realistic description? What is the empirical evidence?

Have these theories been tested?

Because Keynesian theory allows unemployment to persist as a result of the two economic principles of the liquidity trap and rigid wages, they have both been the subject of much testing in the monetarist/Keynesian debate. Econometricians have examined the historical data of a number of countries and over different historical periods.

Liquidity traps, which require exceedingly low interest rates and investment that does not respond to these rates because of negative animal spirit, seem to be rejected by the evidence. Only during the Great Depression, and not in years since then, does a liquidity trap, with people not buying bonds, appear to have occurred.

As for the rigid-wage feature of Keynes's work, the question is not whether actual dollar wages will fall during heavy unemployment; rather, it is whether, with inflation occurring, they will fall in real, inflation-adjusted terms, so as to encourage businessmen to hire more workers at lower and more profitable real wages. With cost-of-living adjustments (COLAs) in wage contracts, this cannot occur, since wages are automatically adjusted to keep pace with inflation.

When cost-of-living adjustments do not occur and wages *do* fall in real terms during an inflationary period, this is called *money illusion*. The evidence of the existence of money illusion that is gained by econometric studies of the response of wages to price levels, shows that money illusion is generally short-term. Money illusion means that workers are fooled or forced into accepting a lower real wage, but it also means that unemployment will eventually disappear as inflation reduces real wages to the point where those wishing to work are hired. With the commitment to full employment since World War II, governments have been unprepared to wait for money illusion to work, and they have risked inflation by stepping in and stimulating demand. The evidence indicates that *the government* has helped prevent wages from declining.

Monetarists have tested their theory by examining the historical relationship between money supplies and prices. Over the long term there is a clear relationship between them.

Is the Keynesian concept of unemployment from deficient private demand consistent with the monetarist explanation?

The unemployment that results from insufficient demand—by leakages exceeding injections—can be accommodated within the monetarists' search theory. However, since demand explanations tend to be associated with Keynesians and search explanations with monetarists, it is unlikely that they will admit that they do often agree. Indeed, their differences are exaggerated by both sides, just so they can form distinct camps. But let's see the way the monetarist and the Keynesian views of unemployment can be reconciled.

How can we combine monetarist and Keynesian theories of unemployment?

In terms of the monetarists' framework of search unemployment, the Keynesian deficient demand means a decline in the number of jobs available. The person searching would tend to find a satisfactory job more slowly if there were less jobs to check out. And more time spent searching—because it's harder to get acceptable offers with fewer opportunities—simply means more unemployment. To add to this, more people are likely to find themselves laid off when there is deficient demand, so even with the same average search time, unemployment would be higher. In terms of our original example, if we move from 1 million to 2 million people losing jobs each month, even with an average search time staying at one month, the average number unemployed at any time will double, from 1 million to 2 million.

We have two theories of unemployment. One says that

people search more, so unemployment is higher when inflation falls short of what is anticipated. The other says unemployment is higher when demand is deficient. In reality, there's truth to both theories. If you are prepared to accept both possibilities as part of a broad theory of unemployment, and can understand what we've said, you'll be closer to the truth than many famous economists are.

Can unemployment ever be zero?

This might seem like a silly question, since you may think that people are always looking for jobs. Some rate of unemployment seems like an inevitable state.

Fewer people would be looking for work if they could check out available jobs more quickly. The fellow who carefully looks around for a couple of months before making his choice does so because he wants to be sure that he doesn't miss a great opportunity. But what if all the available jobs in town were immediately made known to each person who is looking for work? Developments in the communication of information via television could make this possible. A job seeker could turn on his television and have information on all relevant jobs instantly appear on his screen. He could check out salary, fringe benefits, and other important details and make up his mind with a minimum of effort on his part. If less time were spent looking for work, there would be fewer unemployed. We might never reduce the number to zero, but developing job-information systems is a better way of reducing unemployment than controlling aggregate demand by either monetary or fiscal policy. This is because it is so difficult to fine-tune demand and to know where demand should be. We will see this when we examine the monetary-fiscal debate. So let's do this next.

5

CURING OUR ECONOMIC ILLS: MONETARY VERSUS FISCAL POLICY

If all the nation's economists were laid end to end, they would point in all directions.

Anonymous

Another difference between Milton [Friedman] and myself is that everything reminds Milton of the money supply; well, everything reminds me of sex, but I try to keep it out of my papers.

Robert Solow

What is the policy debate?

The debate between the monetarists and the Keynesians revolves as much around the cause of economic ills as around their cure. The biggest question concerns whether the important goals of low inflation and low unemployment can best be achieved through the Federal Reserve System controlling the supply of money, or through the Treasury controlling government spending and taxes. Some economists even question the value of either type of policy and believe that no control is better than some control. This follows either from a feeling that economic policy does not work in a rational world or from a belief that policymakers consciously trying to cure the economic animal could just as easily make the patient worse. If we are to resolve this debate, we must first discover what monetary and fiscal policies are.

What is monetary policy?

This is a tougher question to answer than might first appear to be the case. This is because there are two major contenders as measures of monetary policy and, consequently, two ways of describing what it is. One of these measures is the interest rate and the other is the supply of money. It requires a rather long explanation but we can show that it is safer to stick to a description in terms of the supply of money.

Why should we measure monetary policy by the money supply?

It is often said that monetary policy should be measured by interest rates and that monetary policy is "tight" when interest rates are high. But when will interest rates be high? Interest rates are the payments made to a person or institution for giving up the use of funds for a while. Now, if you expected 6 percent inflation over the next year, and someone—even the government—offered you 5 percent interest, you will be led to say: "When I get back my money with my 5 percent interest, if all prices are 6 percent higher, my money, even with the interest, will buy less than it will buy now." Indeed, if the interest rate is even equal to the inflation rate you expect to occur, you will be left only just as well off after getting back your money as when you gave it up. If you were to receive a small payment—say 2 percent—*after* inflation for letting someone use your money, then with an expected inflation of 6 percent, you might hope to receive 8 percent interest for the use of your money. We know that sometimes you might find this difficult, but within limits, you'll earn higher interest when inflation is expected to be higher. This is because you and everyone else will be demanding more when inflation is expected to be high, and borrowers will be prepared to pay you more because they know that the value of money they will have to repay will be reduced by the anticipated inflation.

In summary, we can say that interest rates will be high when inflation is expected to be high. But when will future inflation be expected to be high? Future inflation can be expected to be high after recent *actual* inflation has been high. We are now in a position to show why high interest rates do not mean monetary policy is "tight", and why we should therefore measure monetary policy by the money supply.

Prices will be rising rapidly when the money supply has also been rising rapidly. We saw this through the quantity theory of money. When prices are rising rapidly, expected inflation will be high and so will the interest rates. Therefore, high interest rates must simply mean that the money supply has been growing rapidly. This is not what we normally think of as a tight monetary policy. High interest rates therefore indicate that monetary policy has been *"easy,"* not that it is currently tight. What is more, this whole situation works in reverse. Low interest rates arise from expectations of low inflation, which means monetary policy has been *"tight,"* not that it is currently easy.

What we have said shows that we cannot use interest rates as a simple measure of monetary policy. If, however, we instead measure monetary policy by the rate of growth of the money supply—whether it be in either the M1s or M2—we will not get into this problem. If the money supply is growing rapidly, monetary policy is expansionary, or easy. If the reverse is true and the money supply is growing slowly, or even shrinking, monetary policy is contractive, or tight. It is that straightforward.

Does the confusion between "tight" and "easy" and high and low interest rates lead to any big mistakes by monetary authorities?

Yes; it causes a terrible mistake. The Federal Reserve System and many other central banks have interpreted—mistakenly, of course—high market interest rates as being a sign that their monetary policy is too tight. Consequently, they have increased the money supply to "ease things up." But as we now know, printing more money just raises prices, and so their action of increasing the money supply raises inflation. And higher inflation raises interest rates. The central banks have interpreted these even higher interest rates as a sign that their monetary policy is too tight, and they again employ the same method: Increase the money supply to ease the apparent shortage of money. In this way the process has continued almost ad nauseum, with higher interest rates causing more money to be printed, thereby raising inflation and making interest rates go higher still.

Fortunately, the error in this merry-go-round scenario is now recognized. Most notably, the recognition took the form of a major shift in monetary-policy focus by the Federal Reserve when its chairman, Paul Volcker, announced in October 1979 that the new monetary targets were to be growth rates in the monetary aggregates, the M1s and M2. Previously, the Fed had attempted to focus on the *federal funds* interest rate, which is the rate that banks charge each other when they exchange their reserves. Even before this major move in the stated focus of the Fed, they had been required to announce their plans for growth in the monetary aggregates over the following year to the U.S. House Banking Committee. These declared targets, which have been given since the mid-1970s, have not, however, been closely followed.

Many other countries' central banks have also moved to the policy of reducing and controlling the growth rate of their money supplies, rather than trying to control the level of interest rates. The Bank of Canada and the Bank of England have gone so far as to announce their targets for many years into the future. But what does this do? We know from the quantity theory that it is supposed to reduce inflation, but what actually occurs?

How does monetary policy work?

If we were to measure monetary policy from the level of interest rates, then the means by which we might describe the mechanism would be straightforward. We would claim that lower interest rates encourage more consumption and investment, because it is cheaper to borrow, and that extra spending means extra income and output. But in what way can we describe the workings of monetary policy measured from changes in the monetary aggregate—that is, the money supply? Do the changes in money supply affect interest rates and thereby affect interest-sensitive consumption and investment, or do they rely on a different mechanism to affect the economy? The answer is that money supply changes have a very direct effect, which comes about because of the way the public reacts to not holding their desired or demanded amounts of cash or money.

What happens when supply and demand for money are unequal?

We have seen that we have a limited demand for money. Suppose we are holding the desired amount of money vis-à-vis the alternative forms of wealth, and suppose that the money supply is then increased. If it helps, we can think of it dropping from a helicopter. If we previously held the desired amount of money, so that the demand equaled the supply, then the supply will exceed demand. This means that we will feel that we have too much money compared to alternative wealth in bonds, stocks, real estate, clothing, antiques, and such. To correct this situation, we will take money and buy bonds, real goods, and such. This creates extra demand. Moreover, money is like a hot potato—we can hand it to somebody else when we spend it, but it still exists and will just circulate around. If the nation's money supply is too large, being more than what people want to hold, then other people who receive it will also spend it. This creates further efforts to move out of money, which raises demand and then prices, as we have seen in the quantity theory.

What happens after prices rise?

When prices have risen by as much as the money supply, there will no longer be an excess supply of money. This is because, with higher prices for what we buy, we need to hold more money just to pay for daily purchases. If, for example, your lunch, the newspaper, and your morning coffee, and your car's gasoline were all to cost twice as much, you'd leave the house in the morning with twice as much money. As prices rise because people spend the excess money, then the newly created money is eventually demanded, and it will all be demanded when prices have risen by the same proportion as the money supply. This is the conclusion of the quantity theory, and we have seen that it comes about because of the efforts by the public to hold their desired amount of money.

What is purchased by the public as it tries to adjust its money balances?

The public could buy anything. To the extent that they buy bonds, this means more funds available to borrowers with lower borrowing costs—that is, lower interst rates. This reduces the opportunity cost of holding money, which, along with the rising prices, works to raise the money demand. In addition, the lower interest rate stimulates business investment. This is the usual notion of the effect of the money supply and is a view that is shared by some Keynesians.

We should note, however, that the excess supply of money could be used directly to buy extra goods, stocks, and such, rather than just bonds. This means that even if interest rates didn't decline, or even if investment is not sensitive to interest-rate declines—two features of Keynesian economics—monetary policy still works. Money exerts direct effects on aggregate demand, as well as indirect effects that work through interest rates and investment.

How does a reduction in money supply work?

A reduction in the money supply—which we might think of as a giant vacuum cleaner in the sky sucking up the money—works to reduce spending. If the supply of money falls below the demand, then to restore the desired amount of money that was previously held, people will sell other assets, such as bonds, stocks, and other things in order to obtain money. This merely redistributes the money; it will not create it. However, it causes declining demand, which lowers prices. When prices have declined as much as the money supply, the lower money supply is sufficient to meet daily purchasing needs, and demand equals supply. We have the quantity theory working in reverse.

What is fiscal policy?

Now that we know that monetary policy should be measured by how rapidly the money supply is growing, with faster growth meaning a more expansionary or easy policy, we can ask the same question about fiscal policy. Well, fiscal policy involves changing government tax revenues and government spending in the hope of affecting the economy. Normally, it is believed—certainly by Keynesians, but not by many monetarists—that reducing taxes or increasing government spending will be expansionary and will stimulate the economy.

How does fiscal policy work?

A cut in taxes will work by leaving people with more income to spend. Income after taxes is called disposable income. Extra disposable income will, as it is spent, perk up total demand. But it goes a lot further than this. If taxes are reduced by granting a $100 rebate, and the people receiving the tax rebate go out and spend, say, $80 of the rebate, someone else in the economy will receive this extra $80—perhaps in addition to their own tax rebate. Since the $80 spent by the first person is extra income to the second person, the second person may go out and spend $64 of this "windfall." The person receiving the $64 will spend some of that amount, and so the process will continue. We can see that the cut in taxes might induce a lot of extra spending—a multiple of the original tax cut—as the effect works its way through the entire economy. This could well explain the saying that, to the government, a couple of billion dollars tax decrease is just a drop in the budget!

An increase in government spending works in essentially the same way as a cut in taxes. If the government goes out and hires extra people to help lower unemployment, these people get income that they would otherwise not have received. When these people spend part of their income—say, $80 of each $100 they earn—a second group will receive it. The second group will spend, say, $64 of each $80 they receive, and again this process will continue, with incomes for the country as a whole rising by a multiple of the original government spending. The extra spending will move through the entire economy, and the multiple by which the total increase in spending exceeds the original spending done by the government is, with great imagination, called *the multiplier.*

How large is the multiplier?

Clearly, since government spending sets off effects that ripple through the economy, creating a multiple expansion of total spending that exceeds the initial injection, the size of this multiplier is important in determining the effect of spending and taxing policies. It should be apparent that the value of extra spending will depend on the *fraction* of the additional income spent.

When the government injects $100.00, let us suppose as we did before that those who receive this spend $80.00, and that the recipients of the $80.00 spend 80 percent of this—or $64.00—and that the recipients of this amount spend 80 percent, or $51.20, and so on. We will have total national spending going up by $100.00 of initial spending, plus $80.00 plus $64.00 plus $51.20, and so on of induced additional spending. The amount of extra spending eventually converges to zero, and at that time total extra spending becomes $500.00. This is not immediately obvious, but if you add $100.00, $80.00, $51.20, $40.96, and so on, you'll see quite quickly that you get close to $500.

Let us now take a different example and suppose that people spend only 50 percent of what they receive in extra income. Then, an initial injection of $100.00 will cause spending at the various steps of $100.00—plus $50.00, plus $25.00, plus $12.50, plus $6.25, and so on. This sum converges to a total of $200.00. The multiplier in our first case is said to be 5, because spending in the economy goes up by $500.00 from an initial injection of $100.00. In the second case, the multiplier is 2.

As previously stated, the crucial element in the size of the multiplier, and therefore in the effectiveness of fiscal policy, is seen to be the fraction of extra income that is spent. This fraction is given the rather grand name of the *marginal propensity to consume*. This is 0.8 when 80 percent of extra income is spent and 0.5 when 50 percent is spent. Since what we do not spend we save, if we spend 80 percent of extra income, we must save 20 percent. We define the *marginal propensity to save* as the fraction of extra income that is saved. It is 0.2 when 80 percent of extra income is spent and 0.5 when only 50 percent is spent.

Once we know the size of the marginal propensities, we also know the size of the multiplier. When the marginal propensity to consume is 0.8 and the marginal propensity to save is 0.2, the government spending multiplier is 5. This is 1.0 divided by the marginal propensity to save of 0.2. When the marginal propensity to consume and to save are 0.5, the government spending multiplier is 2. This is 1.0 divided by the marginal propensity to save of 0.5. In general, the multiplier from government spending is found by dividing the marginal propensity to save into the number 1.0. This makes the marginal propensity to save, and therefore also the propensity to consume, a very important magnitude.

How large is the marginal propensity to consume?

Because the multiplier depends on the marginal propensity to save, which is just 1 minus the marginal propensity to consume, estimating the value of these propensities is an important task. The marginal propensities were used heavily by Keynes in describing his view of the economy and in presenting his proposed fiscal policy cure for the Great Depression. Because of the importance of the propensities, many economists have attempted to measure the amounts. There are two ways to approach the estimation problem. One is to look at surveys of household spending that are conducted and to see how much more income is spent by those with higher income than those with lower income. The other approach is to examine national consumption and national income from the national-income accounts in a number of different successive years. The historical path of consumption and income enables the economist to discover how much of the growth in the national income over the historical period went into additional consumption.

Is there agreement between the results of the two approaches?

Economists who studied budget-survey data gathered by questioning large numbers of households about their income and spending behavior found low marginal propensities to consume—in the region of 0.5. In other words, even though those with higher incomes in the surveys did spend more than those with lower incomes, the extra amount spent (or consumed) was rather small, close to 50 percent of the higher income, which in our examples gives a multiplier of 2. These results were similar to those obtained by studying patterns of income and consumption as they appear through short periods of history. On the other hand, economists who studied how incomes and consumption have moved together over long spans of history found that very high fractions of our growth in income have been consumed, even more than the 0.8 marginal propensity to consume that gave a multiplier of 5 in our example.

Have these results been reconciled?

It was Milton Friedman, in a book called *A Theory of the Consumption Function* (1957), who reconciled the two apparently contradictory sets of results in terms of his *permanent-income hypothesis*. This hypothesis asserts that people do not make consumption decisions on the basis of their income in a current month or year. Rather, they determine what to spend on the basis of what they might earn permanently or normally. When current income and what is normally or permanently earned are the same, there are no problems. However, when you question people about their spending and income, or when you look at a short period of history, there will be people with current incomes that are not normal to them and are therefore not permanent.

What happens when permanent and current income are not equal?

Among people with very high incomes in surveys of budget spending, there will be a large percentage who are doing very well at the time of the survey. That is why they were found in the high-income category. Perhaps they are real estate or automobile salespeople who happen to be enjoying an outstanding month. These people might permanently expect less income than they enjoy at the time of the survey. Consequently, they will spend less out of their current income than someone who would expect that high current income to remain permanent. Similarly, at low-income levels, there will be a high proportion of people who normally do better than they were doing when surveyed. They might be out of work temporarily, with very little income at all, but they will still consume, very possibly more than they are earning. They can do this—at least for a while—by running down their savings. They might do this with the expectation and hope that things should be getting better soon.

What happens in a survey of households, or in a study done over a short interval, is that among low-income earners there will be a relatively large fraction who are earning less than their permanent income. Some low earners could be doing better than usual but there will be more low earners who have unusually low incomes. With consumption tuned to their permanent income, they therefore spend a relatively large fraction of their actual *current*, as opposed to *permanent*, income. Similarly, at high incomes, there will be a relatively large fraction enjoying more current income than they can expect to have permanently. With consumption keyed to the lower permanent income, their consumption will represent a rather small fraction of their actual or current income.

Now we have the bottom line. In a survey of households, we will find that as we look at people with higher and higher incomes, we find more and more with current incomes ahead of permanent income, and who therefore consume a low fraction of current income. They know that things will not continue to be so good permanently. This gives the appearance of people consuming a small fraction of higher incomes, but the effect is an illusion. If incomes were to be permanently higher, the fraction consumed would increase. We should therefore be careful with surveys of households and surveys made over short periods of time. On the other hand, studies conducted over long time spans give better results. Here there isn't a problem of a difference between current and permanent income. Results from long-term studies give the proportion of extra income consumed, which is used in constructing the multiplier. With a marginal propensity to consume of about 0.8, and a marginal propensity to save of about 0.2, we have a multiplier of 5, if everything else is equal.

Everything else is not equal. For one thing, the multiplier exists alongside an economic concept that is known as the *investment accelerator*.

What is the investment accelerator?

To an economist, investment means the production or purchase of plant or capital equipment. Investment is distinct from consumption. Consumption is what we purchase for relatively immediate enjoyment. Investment is what helps us enjoy more in the future, since it enables us to raise production. Buying stocks or bonds is not investment. These are acts of saving, which is the very opposite of investment in that savings is a withdrawal from spending while investment is an injection. Economists therefore use the term investment quite differently than a stockbroker or a banker would.

To the economist, investment in new machines is either to replace those that wear out, which is called *depreciation*, or to increase the number of machines. The latter is called *net investment*. We will be well advised to think in terms of net investment—that is, additions to the number of machines— when we think of the investment accelerator.

The investment accelerator starts from the idea that the total stock of machines that a businessman would like to have will depend on the amount of output he wants to produce. More production means that more machines are required. In fact, we would argue that if a businessman expected to sell twice as much as before, and his firm was at capacity, he would want to have twice his initial number of machines.

If sales and overall demand are constant, the number of machines available should be sufficient, and there will be no need for additional net investment. Net investment will be *zero*. If sales were then to increase, this would mean that more machines are required. While these machines are being produced, *positive* investment is occurring. Once they have been produced, even if sales stay at their higher level, investment will have to *decline*. This follows because once the machines have been produced and acquired, businessmen will have their required number and new machine production can again drop to *zero*. Therefore, if sales increase to a new level and then remain at this level, investment will increase and then decrease. The increased investment has a multiplier effect rather like the government spending multiplier, and so does the decline in investment.

When we combine the multiplier and the accelerator, we can produce very elegant descriptions of a dynamic economy. The dynamics will show ups and downs in production and national income. The multiplier magnifies the swings and gives, with the accelerator, a trade-cycle appearance that is not unrealistic. The dynamics from combined accelerators and multipliers has been described by the Nobel Prize-winning Massachusetts Institute of Technology economist, Paul Samuelson.

With the factors that influence the effect of fiscal policy now explained in terms of multipliers and accelerators, and underlying marginal propensities to consume and to save having been described, we can turn to the measurement of fiscal policy. Since fiscal policy can take the two forms of spending and taxes, we must see how these can be combined.

How do we measure the overall fiscal policy?

Since taxes and government spending are both changing all the time, we usually form a measure of fiscal policy by taking the difference between the government's spending and the taxes it collects. We call this measure the *fiscal-budget deficit*. This is simply government spending minus taxes. When spending exceeds taxes, the government has a deficit. If spending is less than taxes, the government has a surplus, but as we so well know, deficits are more common than surpluses. In measuring fiscal policy, we usually say that the larger the deficit, the more expansionary the fiscal budget is, since a bigger deficit means either higher government spending or lower taxes, both of which should act as stimulants. The advantage of using the budget deficit is that it gives the combined effect of taxes and government spending, so we can interpret the overall effect of fiscal policy. But even in doing this, we have problems in measuring fiscal policy from the resulting fiscal budget deficit. This is true for two reasons, which we will now examine.

Why is the fiscal deficit an imperfect measure
of fiscal policy?

You probably think that if both taxes and government spending were raised by the same amount, there would be no change in government stimulation of the economy. "Surely," you reason, "with the government taking out and handing back equal amounts, it can't have an effect." Well, if you think this, you are wrong—but for a very subtle reason. The fiscal deficit is a poor measure of fiscal policy because the same size of deficit can have different effects. Let us see why.

If your disposable income were reduced by $100 because taxes went up by that amount, you might well reduce the amount you save by $20 and the amount you spend by the remaining $80. This would then work back through the economy. What is important is that an increase in taxes of $100 will reduce initial spending by only $80, with the other $20 showing up as reduced savings. If, however, at the same time, the government raises *its* spending by $100, that will more than compensate for your reduction. The $100 spent by the government is $20 more than the private spending reduction of $80. But recall that the $80 spending cut is the result of a $100 increase in taxes. We can therefore conclude that the net initial effect of raising both taxes and government spending by the same amount is $20 of extra spending. This $20 will then work its way through the entire economy with multiplier effects. We see that if taxes and government spending are both raised by the same amount, even though the fiscal-budget deficit will not change, there is extra stimulation. What is taken as taxes doesn't cut into spending as much as spending is revitalized when the government plows it all back. Indeed, this revitalization of $20 will eventually raise overall spending by the same amount as the original government spending and tax increase, that is, $100. This conclusion, which will take a moment to explain, is called either the *balanced-budget multiplier theorem*, or the *unit-value multiplier theorem*.

What is the balanced-budget multiplier theorem,
or unit-value multiplier theorem?

We recall that the multiplier is 5 when the marginal propensity to consume is 0.8, as in the previous example. Our example also shows that, from a $100 increase in both government spending and taxes (a balanced-budget expansion), we have $20 of extra spending. When this is multiplied by 5, total spending will have gone up by $100. We find that when government spending and taxes are *both raised by the same amount*, total spending rises by this amount, giving us a multiplier of 1, and hence the names balanced-budget multiplier theorem, or unit-value multiplier theorem.

The balanced-budget, or unit, multiplier theorem is valid whatever is the marginal propensity to consume. If the propensity is 0.5, with a multiplier of 2, a tax and government spending increase of $100 will be a total net injection of $50. Why? Because the $100 of extra taxes reduces private spending only $50, compared to the extra government spending of $100. The net injection of $50 with a multiplier of 2 means that total spending rises by $100—again the same as the initial increase in government spending and taxes with a multiplier of 1.

What other reason is there for the fiscal deficit
being a poor measure of fiscal policy?

If there is a large amount of unemployment, as there is during a recession, this itself will work toward creating a fiscal deficit. During periods of heavy unemployment, the government collects less income tax and other taxes because less income is being earned, and it also has to make more expen-

ditures on such things as welfare payments, income mainte-
nance, and unemployment compensation. With less money
coming in from taxes and more money going out because of
the increased expenditures, there will tend to be a fiscal
deficit. But would we say that because of this deficit the government is using expansionary or stimulatory policies? No,
we would not. This deficit is plainly and automatically the
result of unemployment. It is true that the increased government deficit will help stimulate the economy, but this is not
because of any conscious decision by the government. It is a
completely automatic stimulation and, as such, income taxes,
welfare payments, unemployment compensation, and the
like have been dubbed *automatic stabilizers.*

Now, if we can't merely look at the size of the deficit and
say, "Since this is a large deficit, the government is stimulating the economy more than when there is a smaller deficit,"
what *can* we say? We are forced to attempt to discover what
size fiscal-budget deficit there would be in each year *if* there
were no unemployment—that is, if there were full employment. This involves some complex calculations, but if we can
compute the size of the deficit at full employment, we can
say much more. We will know that the deficit we are measuring is not the result of the amount of unemployment that
happens to exist. If we then find one deficit (measured at a
full-employment level) to be bigger than another deficit
(measured at a full-employment level), we can then say this:
When the *full-employment deficit* is bigger, the government is
trying harder to stimulate the economy. Clearly the bigger
deficit is not the automatic result of unemployment, because
we have corrected for that by putting everything on a full-
employment basis.

How do we put the deficit on a full-employment basis?

What is this complex calculation we have mentioned? Well, to put things on a full-employment basis, we have to do the following. We must first work out what tax collections by the government would have been had full employment prevailed. To determine this amount, we must estimate how much the unemployed would have earned and how much taxes they would have paid on these estimated earnings. The amount of total tax collections had full employment occurred is called *full-employment receipts* (or sometimes *high-employment receipts*). If we have some unemployment, we know that actual tax collections will fall short of the full-employment amount.

After figuring out what taxes would have been if full employment had occurred, we must figure out how much the government would have spent under these conditions. We call this *full-employment expenditures* (or sometimes *high-employment expenditures*). If there is some unemployment, we know that the government is spending more than if full employment had occurred. With full employment the government would not be required to pay the unemployed their welfare, unemployment compensation, and so forth.

The full-employment budget deficit is the difference between full-employment expenditures and full-employment receipts. This is what the fiscal-budget deficit would have been had the economy achieved full employment. For example, the full-employment budget could be in surplus when there is an actual deficit. It is said that this sort of accounting is the reason why the government is able to go into the red and be convinced that everything is just rosy. The full-employment budget is, however, the best measure of the strength of the government's determination to stimulate the economy.

Fortunately for us, there are plenty of people who are

willing to make the complex calculations that are required for computing the full-employment deficit. All we need to do is find it in a bank report, a newspaper, or in the annual statement of the President's Council of Economic Advisors. Most people talk about the ordinary deficit because they don't understand the often more meaningful full-employment deficit. You can now really stun these people with your knowledge of the more appropriate way to measure the strength of fiscal action.

Is the budget deficit, based on full employment or otherwise, the only deficit we hear about?

No. We also hear a lot about the balance-of-payments deficit. This is defined as the difference between earnings from abroad (from exports, sales of bonds, and the like) on the one hand, and payments made to other countries (for imports, foreign stocks and bonds, and the like) on the other hand. The balance-of-payments deficit is a totally different concept from the fiscal-budget deficit, and the two should not be confused.

Are all the taxes that we pay included in actual measures of fiscal policy?

All the taxes we *see* are included in government receipts, but there is a very, very important tax that we do *not* see. We have already seen this other tax in our story about the fruit tree and our Englishman enjoying his remarkably cheap vacation on the agreeable Aegean island. Since it appeared in chapter 4, there is no need to review it here. But we should note that the inflation tax is paid by all of us, even though it never appears on our income tax forms, and most of us don't live on vacation islands visited by unquestionably honest Englishmen.

Just as monetary policy can constitute a hidden tax, there are dangers inherent in fiscal policy. It is very tempting for the government to try to "spend its way out of a recession" by increasing its purchases and the number of people it employs to help stimulate demand. It is an unfortunate attribute of the nature of government, however, that it finds it much more difficult to fire than to hire. As a result, when a recession is over and demand is rising entirely on its own, the government does not scale down its spending. It's rather like a ratchet; there is no reverse.

What does the evidence show about monetary versus fiscal policy?

There have been numerous attempts to provide convincing evidence on the policy debate, and these attempts have involved literally thousands of economists, statisticians, and econometricians. The most common form of evidence comes from an examination of economic statistics from the post–World War II period. Some economists have looked farther back in history, but regular collection of economic *time-series* data on inflation, unemployment, and such is scantier in earlier periods. A variety of very sophisticated—and some not-so-sophisticated—econometric techniques have been applied to the statistics within a variety of models to see what policy events best explain the path that the economy has followed. Different studies yield different conclusions, but some merit has been found in both types of policy for influencing real GNP. It is fair to say that the best empirical studies show that printing more money, reducing taxes, and increasing government spending can all contribute to lowering unemployment. Over long periods of history, there is general agreement that inflation is affected largely by the money supply, but there is considerable disagreement over how quickly this occurs.

How long does it take for monetary and fiscal policy to work?

One reason why it's so difficult to find agreement on which type of policy has the greatest effect is that the economy does not react immediately when the policies are put into effect. What is more, there are many other changes taking place at any particular time. It therefore becomes difficult to associate the change in a policy and the change in direction of the economy. Nevertheless, by studying a long enough period of history to see which policy decisions preceded major changes in the economy, we can obtain some idea of how long it is before policies begin to take effect.

It is generally felt that monetary policy works with a long and relatively variable lag and that effects on real GNP or unemployment do not show up for at least six months. Any effect on prices of a change in the growth of the money supply takes more than a year, with the peak effect at eighteen months. Fiscal policy appears to have a shorter lag, perhaps as short as a couple of months, with government spending increases showing up quickly in the spending for the rest of the economy. But not everyone will agree with these conclusions, and some economists even challenge whether policies work at all.

Which economists believe that macroeconomic policies don't work at all?

We have already said that monetarists question the effectiveness of fiscal policy and that Keynesians question monetary policy. But there are other economists who question macroeconomic policies on grounds other than their monetarist or Keynesian colors.

Some economists believe that fiscal policies will not work since government spending will merely *crowd out* the private sector. In concrete terms, crowding out means that there are only so many factors of production in existence, and if the government uses them, they can't be used by the private sector. Crowding out occurs by bidding up factor prices or interest rates. For example, if the government runs a fiscal deficit in order to spend more, and it finances the deficit by selling bonds, this will raise interest rates. This discourages private investment, which frees up the factors of production to move from the private to the government sector.

The rational-expectations economists, whom we spoke of earlier, believe that monetary policy cannot effect unemployment. Their argument is that if expectations of workers are rational, then they can't be fooled for long by inflation. You will recall that monetary policy could reduce unemployment if the inflation it created caused workers to accept jobs more quickly. However, when workers are rational and do not have illusions about dollar amounts as opposed to real amounts of wages, inflation, and hence monetary policy, will not lower unemployment. As a result, believers in rational expectations even question changing monetary policy, and they frequently suggest that the Federal Reserve should be instructed to ensure that the money supply grows at a constant rate, say, 4 percent per year, and should not take discretionary actions.

Milton Friedman, a believer in monetary policy, reached

the conclusion of the rational-expectations people a long time ago. However, he was in favor of having a constant growth rate of the monetary aggregate for a different reason. He believes that the Fed has so much power but knows so little about its effect that it is just as likely to make things worse as it is to make them better. It is therefore safer for the Fed to stay out of discretionary policy endeavors and, instead, to keep to mechanical targets. This is an interesting situation: We have the believers in rational expectations who don't believe that monetary policy works, and Milton Friedman who believes it works very well, both reach the same conclusion, that is, discretionary monetary policy should not be used.

There are people who will go beyond saying that macroeconomic policies don't work. They claim that they work in reverse and that, for example, rising interest rates can actually raise inflation and the national product.

Can rising interest rates increase inflation and the national product?

We have emphasized that the growth rate in the money supply, and not interest rates, should be used in the measurement of monetary policy. Nevertheless, it would normally be believed that rising interest rates would slow down the economy and eventually slow inflation. Despite this, some economists argue that rising interest rates raise the cost of doing business and the cost of mortgage debt on housing. As the costs rise, so do prices and price indexes. It follows, according to this argument, that rising interest rates raise inflation.

There is some truth in this argument, but it is a short-run effect. High interest rates that reduce demand *are* deflationary, that is, they will slow the rate of inflation. However, as the rates go up, they raise costs of living as measured by most basket-weighted price indexes, such as the CPI. Once they have ceased rising and are at a higher level, they will reduce demand and inflation. The perverse effect is temporary.

The effect of rising interest on real national product, which looks perverse, is more subtle than the effect on the rate of inflation. It is claimed by some noneconomists that when interest rates are high, there is an incentive for manufacturers to deliver goods quickly. The quicker they deliver, the quicker they are paid, and the quicker they can repay debt or earn interest. Since many goods are sold to order, when orders have already been given and interest rates go up, it causes delivery or shipments to go up. This will show up as a temporary increase in the real national product.

This case is not implausible. I do not know of careful econometric testing of it, but casual observation of statistics and certain stories bear it out. For example, when interest rates rose sharply in October 1979, shipments and deliveries were very high in the following two months. Even construction activity picked up as contractors who would be paid on completion of jobs speeded up their work. There are stories of complaints by clothing stores that apparel manufacturers were delivering summer styles in December, up to two months early, causing havoc with storage space because spring clothing was still unsold. It was only in March 1980 that the slowdown in demand and shipments began to show. But does the slowdown in demand also slow inflation?

Will a recession cool inflation?

In macroeconomic policy analysis it is hard to find two economists who agree. There are skeptics who claim that recessions don't cool down inflation. Others believe that a serious recession will reduce inflation, but that the cost is too high. A former chairman of the President's Council of Economic Advisers, Arthur Okun, said that using a recession to cool inflation is like burning down the house to bake a loaf of bread.

Recessions will bring down inflation. During the Great Depression, prices—and the supply of money—fell more than 30 percent. During the short but severe recession of 1974–1975, inflation fell from double digits to less than 5 percent. Smaller economic slowdowns have smaller effects. The scale of recession we are prepared to tolerate is not too likely to lower the price level—that is, make prices decline. However, they will bring down the rate at which prices are rising. Remember that slower inflation still allows prices to rise. If we allow a reduction in aggregate demand, it doesn't have to be too severe to induce people to raise prices by a lower amount than they had been raising them. Not every economist will agree.

While there is no great agreement on the effectiveness or wisdom of macroeconomic policy, there are some things about which many economists will agree. Among these are the important objectives of economic policy.

6

RELEVANT OBJECTIVES: JOBS, OUTPUT, AND INFLATION

I do not like work even when someone else does it.

Mark Twain

Are jobs the first priority of good economic policy?

Listen to some economists and to just about everyone employed by a labor union, and you'll get the feeling that jobs are what really matter. The sort of comment that you will frequently hear is that with such-and-such a number of new people entering the labor force, it is the government's obligation to adopt policies to ensure that they all have work. At other times you'll hear that competition from cheaply made foreign footwear or television sets is undermining American jobs. These jobs, it might often be said, should be protected by keeping the foreign products out of this country through tariffs or restrictive quotas.

The truth of the matter is that we want the products of the jobs, not the jobs themselves. We want the fruits and steaks that come from the labor on our farms. We want the products of effort at the auto plants. We want the hamburgers and shirts, the clean clothes, and the television shows. Sure, some of us like our jobs. I think mine is great. But if the products available to us were so plentiful that we could enjoy the freedom to work fewer hours and could spend our time doing what we pleased, would that not be a better world? Of course it would.

Our national well-being is not determined by whether we all have jobs. It is determined instead by the amount we produce for each of us to enjoy—our per capita real GNP. With today's productivity in the United States, even with 10 or 20 percent of the population without any work, we would almost all be better off than in a fully employed India or Pakistan. That is because we produce more per person in this country. It is not because we have more jobs.

Having accepted that it is not jobs that should count, but rather the available output of goods and services, a few controversial questions turn out to have very clear answers. We can now look at some of these controversial questions.

Should we protect jobs with import duties and quotas on cheap foreign goods?

Tariff and quota protection of domestic firms from keen competition from abroad has often been defended on the grounds that, without the protection, jobs in the U.S. firms would be lost. Indeed, there is no question that those who are displaced by foreign competition will experience a great loss. But, collectively as a nation, are we not better off being in a position to enjoy plentiful footwear, television sets, cars, and steel that other countries can produce more cheaply than we can? A strong case can be made for enjoying the goods that others produce comparatively cheaply so that we can specialize in products that we make well.

Since as a nation we can have more and cheaper goods and services by not having tariffs and quotas on imports, we can use some of these gains to help retrain and relocate those who do lose their jobs. The displaced workers can be encouraged to move into jobs making products that are competitive throughout the world. The earnings from their exports can then pay for the imports. This way we can have more goods and, with everybody retrained, no fewer jobs.

Should we create new jobs by accelerating the rate at which older workers retire?

More than once—especially during times of heavy unemployment—it has been suggested that older workers leave their jobs early to make room for the young. But as a nation, can this make us any better off? Can we have a larger amount of goods and services to enjoy collectively if we remove skilled and seasoned workers and replace them with workers who are as yet untrained? No; if anything, the national output would decline. We need to ensure that there are no hindrances that interfere with the ability of the young to find jobs while the older and experienced vital employees continue to work.

What hindrances are there to the young finding jobs?

One potential hindrance to obtaining work for the young and less skilled lies in the minimum-wage laws. There is no question that minimum-wage laws have been erected and protected in the past by well-meaning people who genuinely have the interests of the workers at heart. And, indeed, for those who do get the jobs that offer more than they would otherwise, the minimum-wage laws have been a help. But what of the rest who are not hired because of the law? How can this occur? It is not difficult to see how.

Suppose an employer has a job that is worth $2 an hour to get done. Perhaps it involves pumping the customer's gas and cleaning windshields in a service station or perhaps tidying up an office floor at the end of the day. But what if the law says that the employer has to pay $4 an hour for that work? The service station owner will find it to his advantage to switch to self-service gas pumps, and the office manager might buy an expensive industrial vacuum cleaner and do the tidying up himself. You might well feel that demeaning work deserves $4 an hour—or even more—for menial jobs are certainly not much fun. But what about the person who would be prepared to pump gas at the service station for $2 an hour while going through college, or a mother who would be happy to add a little to her income with a part-time cleaning job? Minimum-wage laws leave some of these people unemployed and without the choice of working for less if they wish to do so.

Can we all enjoy a rosier future by raising our social security or pension contributions?

Going back to our fundamental rule that it is the national output that determines our collective standard of living, we can pause and ask another question, this time about retirement pension plans. We will see how easy it is to forget the primary importance of output when the context is just slightly changed.

It is true that the more preparations any person makes for

future retirement, the better his or her standard of living will be during that retirement. But can we all collectively provide for future consumption and an easy retirement? Clearly, the collective living standard of all of us in the future, just as today, will depend on the collective output there will be to enjoy. And this is all. We do not necessarily add to the future national output when we contribute to pension and social security plans. The number of goods retirees will enjoy in the future will depend on the output of those who are producing at that time. Big pension plans can help those who have them to spend, but only at the expense of those doing the work. Savings in general can raise future output by helping provide more efficient capital for future generations to use in their production effort, but there is no guarantee that this is what social security and pension contributions will provide.

Can this be explained differently?

We can put all of this in a slightly different way. It is not uncommon to hear the argument that, with population control, we can all enjoy better lives in the future. It is true that the earth provides rather limited space and that many resources are not in infinite supply. But we cannot move too quickly toward reducing average family size. Ask yourself this. If the generation that will one day retire does not have many children and productivity does not grow, who will provide the output that we will all require, and how can any amount of pension funds help us to provide it? Output is the fundamental force behind living standards, although it is very easy to forget this and to let our thinking stray.

With output being so important, what makes some countries so rich in output while others are so poor? Is it good fortune?

What is the cause of the wealth of nations?

Those people who are lucky enough to live in the richer countries of the world enjoy a relatively high standard of living, not just as a result of their own efforts, but because their ancestors were able to leave them more capital on which to build their own fortunes. There are individuals in the poorer, less-developed countries who are just as intelligent and just as strong as those in developed nations, and yet their living standards are much lower.

Countries, like people, can inherit their wealth, or they can earn it. But as anyone who starts with very little knows, it is difficult to get rich if you have no base on which to build, even if you are prepared to work hard and long. There is a vicious circle of poverty for poor people. Because they are poor, they cannot afford a good education and cannot take the time to develop skills or a capital base; and because they have no skills or capital, they remain poor. The viciousness of this circle of individual poverty is no less wicked when it is applied to nations as a whole. Poor countries do not have resources, capital, or skills. And because they are poor, they cannot afford to build schools to train their people or to build roads and factories to produce more goods. And so the next generation remains poor.

Are natural resources essential to wealth?

North America is abundant in natural resources, even though we all know only too well that critical shortages of some items do exist. There is a mass of space and good agricultural land, and it is far from uncommon for visiting Europeans to be overwhelmed by the amount of land that isn't used for agriculture or other productive purposes. North America is also rich in coal and minerals, trees, fish, and much more. But wealth does not require natural resources, although, of course, it helps to have them. At least as important a national resource are the people, and an intelligent, healthy, well-trained, and well-motivated population can by itself produce great wealth. There are numerous examples of industrious people achieving great economic success without a natural-resource base. We can look at Germany and Japan, Singapore and Hong Kong, where the growth rates in the latter half of the twentieth century have overshadowed those of the countries rich in natural resources.

National output requires national input. The essentials are raw materials, labor, capital—and the knowledge and managerial skills to use these effectively which is summarized by the technology that is available. Raw materials can be bought on world markets, although it is no disadvantage to have them available at home. A nation can build its wealth on its people, its machines, and its technological know-how. But the people must be trained and the machines must be built. A country that hovers near the subsistence level cannot afford to have people of prime age sitting in school instead of producing what they must eat. The productivity of workers in the richer countries is high enough to produce a surplus, which feeds the many teenagers and young adults who are learning productive skills. The output of such workers is high because they have skills. So, because the country is rich in skills, it can afford to create more skills. What is true for education is also true for capital and machines. Investing means not consuming some of what we are currently producing, but this can be done only if there is surplus that can be set aside. Poor nations do not have this surplus and so they continue to remain poor.

How can we help poor nations along the path to development?

People have begun talking of a new economic order. When poor countries, with starving millions, have a nuclear potential, we could all be forced to share what we now enjoy. This is a theme taken up by Robert Heilbroner, one of the broader thinking economists of today. Some of us have been singularly lucky in the past. We might consider sharing our luck a little more, or some day we may have no choice in the matter.

Development economists study the best way to help the poor nations out of their economic plights. Clearly, a surplus must be created so that they can train their young and put a little capital aside for a later day. This surplus might have to be borrowed or given to them in some way. Gifts, loans, agreements to buy, and other forms of development aid exist, but the gap between the rich and the poor seems difficult to close. And it should go without saying that it is not jobs that the poor nations need, but rather it is the ability to raise the productivity of those who work. It is output that is in critically short supply, not jobs.

If output is an important goal of economic policy, then surely keeping inflation under control is also important. But the reason for this is not that inflation is harmful for the overall economy, but that those who lose from inflation are the ones who can least afford to be hurt.

Who loses from inflation?

Your first reaction might be that we all lose. You might believe that older people on fixed incomes from pensions or life-insurance annuities lose the most, but it probably seems that we must all lose. Well, in actual fact, there are probably as many gainers as losers. The problem is that we don't always admit the gains. These gains—and losses—come from unanticipated inflation.

Why is anticipated inflation different from unanticipated inflation?

We can think of two important kinds of inflation—the inflation that people anticipate and the inflation they don't. The first type—the anticipated inflation—is really of very little trouble to us. If we can anticipate the degree of inflation that is going to occur, we will demand to be compensated for the erosion of our purchasing power. If we are making a loan or buying a bond, we will expect to receive compensation for the expected inflation that is reflected in the size of the interest rates that we are paid. Furthermore, the payer of interest knows that he will be repaying the loan in dollars with less buying power, so he will not mind having to pay more interest.

Similarly, in wage bargaining, to the extent that inflation is likely to occur over the contract period, workers will demand extra pay, and employers are likely to agree, knowing that the inflation makes the real wages he is paying that much less. Even annuities and pensions can have provisions built in if the rate of inflation that is to occur is known in advance.

Unfortunately, the amount of inflation isn't generally known in advance. As a result, the actual rate that occurs often exceeds, or perhaps falls short of, what people thought would happen. This type of inflation—unanticipated inflation—is the worst kind. But we will see that even though a lot of people suffer from unanticipated inflation, there are also some who gain. Let us show this by considering:

What happens when inflation is greater than anticipated?

Those people who have loaned out money—the creditors—will lose from inflation that exceeds the anticipated value. Even if they succeed in getting a sufficiently high interest rate to compensate them for the price rises they anticipated, this will not be enough to compensate for inflation that exceeds this amount. This includes people who hold assets such as bonds purchased during low anticipated inflation. If you hold any of these bonds, you will have discovered this for yourself.

But what about the issuers of the bonds and other debts? What happens to the amount that they owe after they discover that inflation has eaten into what they must repay? Debtors—those who owe money—achieve a positive gain from unanticipated inflation. Moreover, their gain is one that offsets the losses of the creditors to whom the debtors owe the money. The debtors' gain is the creditors' loss. Economists refer to this as a real-income redistribution, or a transfer within a zero-sum game in which gains equal losses.

Who are these debtors who gain from inflation?
Are they a select group of clever businessmen?

The gainers are not an especially select group; they include anyone who owes money on a home mortgage or has a
car loan. For these people, inflation in excess of anticipated
values—which is therefore not reflected in the interest
rate—makes for loan repayments that are easier to bear. The
loan payments represent a smaller and smaller fraction of income. This is no consolation for those who didn't buy a
home and take out a nice, cheap, fixed-interest mortgage,
but it does give an indication of how large a group would
reap positive benefits from unanticipated inflation.

Mortgages and auto loans are a relatively small fraction of
total debt. The biggest debtor in virtually every nation is the
government. Their debt—the national debt—is held by the
citizens in the form of many treasury bills and bonds. As inflation occurs, the buying power of the face value of what
the bondholders and billholders have in their hands erodes.
And their loss is the government's gain; it can repay its debt
in cheap dollars, whose value has been beaten down by
inflation.

But who gains if the government gains?

The government, it is hoped, is the representative of the
people. If the government gains because it owes dollars that
are worth less, then, in some kind of way, a group of people
must gain because the government's debt is the people's
debt. We have seen that government bondholders lose. The
gainers, therefore, are the other group that provides money

to the government—the taxpayers. Or, more precisely, they are *potential* gainers.

Some people would believe that the government's gain would leave taxes unaffected and would, instead, allow more government waste. Whatever you believe, you can see how complex the gainers-versus-losers process can become.

Do businesses also gain?

Businesses issue bonds that make them debtors to the people who buy them. These are the corporate bonds that constitute one way by which businesses raise money to finance their spending plans. To the extent that businesses are net debtors, they gain from unanticipated inflation. But businesses also buy bonds from other businesses and from the government. They also make loans to the public; banks are a business. This can make businesses net creditors, causing them to lose from unanticipated inflation. It turns out, from numerous studies that have been made, that about as many businesses are net debtors as are net creditors. Consequently, as a group, businesses do not gain from any other group, such as consumers, from unanticipated inflation. Some gain and some lose and, overall, it's a zero-sum game.

So why is there such a great hullabaloo about inflation?

Past inflation is history. As we survive those periods, we either gain or lose and can at least feel happy about the fact that we survived. What hurts us all—each and every one of us—is not the inflation that we know and have seen, but the inflation we don't know and that we are *about* to see. It is the uncertainty that lies ahead that frightens all of us.

It is little consolation that the unseen inflation *could* make you better off (if you own a mortgaged home, for example). Most of us would rather avoid playing the risky game of inflation. Inflation is bad if it is unpredictable and might wipe out our savings, even though it might just as easily make us better off. Most people do not realize this and simply think that inflation is just plain bad, no matter how you look at it. It is, but only because we don't know how extensive it will be and on which side of the fence it will leave us—compared to someone else.

Can inflation indexing provide a solution?

If it is uncertainty about inflation that is the real culprit in our lives, then indexing of economic contracts becomes a highly valuable practice that we should encourage. Indexing means paying more back to creditors the more prices rise. Thus, if the rate of inflation is low, they will get little compensation; if it is high, they will get a lot. That way, the prospect of uncertain future inflation becomes much easier to bear. Creditors know they will not lose, and pensioners, for example, know that they can continue to pay the rent and utility and grocery bills. We all end up with considerably more peace of mind.

Cost-of-living adjustments—a form of indexing—are already common in wage-contract settlements. It is in the area of financial contracts and pension planning that indexing needs to be done.

How about indexing the income tax?

When our incomes rise because of inflation, and by the same amount as inflation, we are no better off—before taxes. However, our inflated incomes can force us into higher and higher tax brackets. The income tax structure is progressive, which means that the rich should pay a bigger fraction of their income in taxes. (Loopholes often make the opposite the case—that is, taxes become regressive with the rich paying out a smaller fraction—which is why the loopholes should be closed.) Because of the progressive nature of taxes, we end up worse off from inflation after taxes have been taken out. As incomes inflate with prices, the higher tax brackets in which we find ourselves force us to pay out a bigger fraction of our overall income to Uncle Sam.

Many countries have indexed tax brackets and lump-sum deductions and exemptions. These countries increase the amount of income needed to get into each tax bracket by the amount of inflation that has occurred. If inflation ran at a rate of 10 percent over the previous year, every dollar value on the tax schedule is raised by 10 percent. That way, a taxpayer enters a higher tax bracket only when his real income becomes higher, and he is not impoverished by a higher inflation-induced tax bite. It is a very good idea to index the tax schedule; if this is not done, the government winds up with a bigger share of the action each year that there is inflation. That doesn't give the government much incentive to break the inflationary cycle. It continues to gain from printing the money that causes inflation and then from the inflation itself as more taxes are collected.

*Won't indexing make it hard to break out
of an inflationary situation?*

It is true that if we pay people more because prices go up, this might cause more inflation, followed by more wage increases, and so on. But the process does have its limits. We know from the quantity theory of money that you can't pay a truckload of money for a newspaper unless there are mountains of money, or if the truckloads of money move fast enough to be available for everyone to buy their paper and everything else they want. If we control the quantity of money and the rate at which that quantity expands, indexing might slow us down in curbing inflation, but it will not prevent us from eventually getting it cured.

Indexing can help reduce the worry of uncertain inflation while we attempt to bring it under control by reducing the growth rate of the nation's money supply. But even if the problem of inflation is solved, we still have to deal with economic booms and busts.

7

ECONOMICS OF BOOMS AND BUSTS

An economist is a person who has one foot in the oven and the other in the freezer and says, "On the average, things aren't too bad."

Anonymous

Economists are always half right in their forecasts. But they don't know which half it will be.

Anonymous

Are business cycles a wave of the past?

What of the regular ups and downs that used to be known as the *business,* or *trade, cycle?* In our discussion of macroeconomics, we have made little mention of the repetitive and apparently unavoidable rythmic cycles that the economy used to follow.

Ups and downs in economic activity do still occur, but economists of all shades tend to agree that the wider swings are being prevented. This is attributed to *automatic stabilizers* that increased government spending and taxes have brought about—even if incidentally—and which deserve a reexamination, even though they were discussed before in connection with fiscal policy.

Have automatic stabilizers eliminated cycles?

It must seem like small consolation for the massive bite that income taxes can take from the reward for work, but these income taxes do help keep the economy on an even keel. If the economy swings down and employment and activity begin to slide, the amount the government collects in taxes also begins to decline. By removing less from the pockets of those who possess the power to spend, the reduced taxes help hold up the level of demand. But even this is not all.

The other side of the government's ability to tax is its ability to spend, and we know that the ability to spend can easily exceed the ability to tax, the difference being the fiscal-budget deficit. The government's tendency to spend, however, does augment the effect of taxes when it comes to keeping the economy on a steady course. As we saw earlier, in an economy on the decline, the government is required to provide payments to certain groups through unemployment compensation, welfare payments, and the like. The extra amount that the government spends in this way helps to maintain demand and keep the economy sailing along. The reverse should occur as things get overheated and the economy is doing "too well," although there is a lack of symmetry here; federal budget surpluses do not seem to flow so easily from a economy that is doing well.

What does a legally required balanced budget mean for the automatic stabilizers?

Legally required balanced budgets certainly prevent the government from spending more than it receives in taxes. A permanently balanced budget, however, does mean that the automatic stabilizers would be hampered.

There is an alternative course, however, that could be followed and that would preserve the stabilizers and still keep the government under restraint. Instead of balancing the actual budget, the federal government could be required to maintain a balance in the *high*, or *full-employment*, amount. The high, or full-employment, budget, which (as we know) is the amount of deficit that would exist if the economy were at full employment, can be kept in balance at all times without precluding required *actual* deficits—from more spending and lower taxes—when times are hard. Some economists, however, argue that rather than worry about the budget deficits, in full-employment form or otherwise, the government should maintain the real value of national debt. The logic behind this, which involves the national debt being retired by inflation, isn't straightforward, so we shall start by explaining what we mean by national debt.

What is the national debt?

The national, or public, debt comes from past fiscal-budget deficits. The Treasury can finance spending that exceeds revenues by selling treasury bills and bonds. These are purchased by the public and the central bank. Over the years, more and more deficits means more and more of these treasury bills and bonds being held. This is the national, or public, debt, which is more than $3,000 for the average American.

The national debt is increased when the Treasury experiences deficits because more bills and bonds must be sold. It is reduced when there is a surplus. This straightforward accounting is fine when there is no inflation, but it needs to be reexamined when prices are rising quickly. This is because the real national debt is retired by either having fiscal surpluses and using the funds to repurchase the treasury bills and bonds or by having rapid inflation. The inflation rate involves reducing the real debt burden, so we should explain the nature of the burden.

What is the burden of the national debt?

The burden of the debt is often said to be the interest that must be paid to debt holders. We must remember, however, that the national debt is both owed and owned. To the extent that we are paying the interest to other citizens—the ones who hold the treasury bills and bonds—we are taking from Peter to pay Paul. When foreigners hold the treasury bills or bonds, it is more complicated, but, generally, the payment of interest on the national debt cannot be considered an overall burden. The debt is an asset to some and a liability to others.

When there is inflation, the real value of outstanding treasury bills and bonds will fall, since their stated dollar or nominal face values will not purchase as much as before. Some economists argue that this gives the government a different objective—to keep the real debt from increasing. This is very easily achieved with fiscal deficits by allowing inflation to reduce the real purchasing power of the treasury bills and bonds. With a national debt of $3,000 per person, and inflation at 10 percent, the real debt is reduced by $300 per person each year. As long as the government keeps its additional fiscal deficits below $300 per person per year, the *real* value of the outstanding national debt will decline despite the additional deficits.

But who gains from reducing the national debt?

Holders of the national debt find that inflation robs them of buying power. The holders' burden is the gain of the rest of the nation. This, however, doesn't mean that the effects of the national debt cancel each other, leaving no overall real economic effects. When the government is borrowing, there is a reduction in funds available for private investment. This is what we have called a crowding-out effect. The growth in the formation of the private capital stock is reduced, and this lowers the growth of the future national income. In addition, the taxes required to service extra national debt could work as a disincentive to those who must pay them.

This account should show that the effect of the national debt isn't straightforward. The interest burden is offset from one group to another. A real burden does remain because of capital stock and work disincentive effects. Nevertheless, more frightening than the consequence of a large national debt is the consequence of a dramatic decline in national income.

Will we recognize the crunch when it comes?

There was no mistaking the Great Depression of the early 1930s when that came. Apart from seeing mass layoffs, terrible economic suffering, and—in some places—more than 20 percent of the work force unemployed, there was a rash of bank failures, the volume of which had never before been seen. In just a few years, 8,000 banks had failed.

But would downturns follow a similar course if they were to come again? The simple answer to this is no, but to see why, we should quickly peer back at the running of a bank.

Why did so many banks fail in the Great Depression?

Our banks, as we have seen, are run on the principle of a fractional reserve. Bank reserves, which are largely kept with the central bank—the Fed—are required to exceed or meet a minimum fraction of the value of the bank's customers' deposits. The consequence of this is that the bank, at any time, has at its immediate disposal only a fraction of what it owes. If all of the customers were to go to their bank on the same day and demand that it give back all it owes them, the bank would be unable to do so. But that is no problem.

Banks work on the accurate presumption that we are all unlikely to go to the bank at the same time. Indeed, much of the bank's deposits lie untouched year after year. The bank knows this and therefore puts most of its deposits to work. It makes loans to business and government by buying their bills and bonds. It makes loans to consumers who want to buy vehicles and homes. It keeps back a fraction to satisfy those who do come in and demand their funds, and this fraction is what is protected by banking law. But the bulk of their money is loaned out and is earning the bank interest on each and every day.

With a fraction as reserves and the rest out in loans, the bank does have assets to back all that it owes, and even some on top of that. It's just that it doesn't have it all there in ready cash. It can take some time to call in all its loans if it ever does have an urgent need for funds.

Now we can explain why so many banks failed during the Great Depression. After an initial major bank failure in Europe and a failure in the United States, large groups of people began to wonder about the safety of their own banks. Just to be sure that they would not lose their deposits, they ran to their bank. As solvent as the banks may have been, they were not able to immediately meet the demands of all those who came. But as more and more banks were forced to close their doors, the more other banks were suspected by their depositors. A trickle of doubt became a river of panic as bank after bank was forced to close its doors. Yet the assets were always there. It just took time to convert the less liquid assets into the cash that was demanded by the nervous bank customers.

Could bank panics happen again?

A bank panic of the variety experienced in the Great Depression can no longer occur. Since 1933 United States bank deposits have been protected by the Federal Deposit Insurance Corporation (FDIC). The FDIC will make good, up to $100,000 as of 1980, any loss a depositor incurs, and many other countries have similar insurance schemes. That's all it takes to avoid another mad surge. If we all feel secure, we will not rush to the bank. If *we* don't rush to the bank, then no one else will begin to feel insecure. Bank failures thus become very rare events and are not a feature of an economic decline. But if a slump will not be marked by runs on the banks, how can we tell when one is about to occur?

What are the economic predictors of a downturn?

In reality, there is no simple way of spotting an economic downturn early on. There are indexes of leading indicators that are supposed to work, and these involve various components that are each supposed to be related to the major economic variables. The forecasters look at building permits, orders for capital equipment, stock prices, credit advanced, and much more. But even the indexes produced from these can miss the important changes in conditions until they have already occurred. Some of the components of the indexes—especially the inventory patterns—even work in reverse.

One of the more reliable indicators of the level of economic activity is provided by the private Conference Board. Every month the Conference Board gathers together the numbers of job listings that are advertised in the major employment centers of the country. They then maintain an often-quoted index that gives an idea of whether the job listings are rising or declining. There appears to be a consistent lag of around four months between a decline in job offerings and a decline in the level of employment.

What other predictors are there?

A leading indicator, such as the job-opening index, is a much more valuable predictor of the economy than an index based on the past. The Federal Reserve Board publishes an index of industrial output for each month, but this only serves to tell us where we've been and not where we are going. The same is true of unemployment, layoffs, national income and product, retail sales, and the rest. Housing starts do provide an indication of future employment trends, because over a period of months the number of building-trade workers employed in building the house increases. Indeed, if we know where the data could be found, the number of architects that are unemployed would give an indication of trends even before the housing-starts data begin to change. However, as things stand, we never know the future as well as we, the forecasters, indicate.

It is said that rising inventories of goods on hand is a powerful sign that business confidence is high and that the economy is about to advance. These inventories are presumed to indicate that the firm is readying itself for strong future sales, and the inventories are held to meet the great demands that are anticipated. But the actual situation could be the complete reverse. Inventories can grow only if firms produce more than they sell. Indeed, by definition, the change in goods on hand equals volume produced minus volume sold. If sales have begun an unpredicted decline, then some goods will go unsold and the inventories—the unsold goods on hand—will therefore rise. This is very definitely not a good sign. We discover that high inventory stocks might just as well mean that sales have declined as that business confidence is high, with future demand expected to rise. Such signs can point up when we are on the way down. That is the sorrowful state of a vast number of economic forecasts, and it is why not all recessions and depressions arrive when expected.

When is a recession not a depression?

It has been said that when your friend is unemployed, it is a recession, and when it is yourself, it is a depression. Recessions, however, are the milder, more recent phenomena. As the 1940s slid into the 1950s and the 1950s rolled into the 1960s, economic progress became the accepted and expected norm. Standards of living grew in almost every year, and the prospect of any sustained decline in these standards seemed less and less within the realm of possibility. With the economic calamity of the Great Depression of 1929–1933 further and further removed, a new word was needed to describe any temporary faltering in the rate of progress. The word *recession* emerged as a description for these milder, modern conditions. If depression is to describe an extreme reduction in the level of our national output, then recession can describe a small reduction that does not persist. In actual fact, recessions are formally identified and given their label by the National Bureau of Economic Research (NBER) that is currently headed by Martin Feldstein of Harvard University. Many people believe that a recession is two successive calendar quarters of negative growth in the real GNP. This, in fact, is inaccurate. The NBER looks at much more than this. It requires a vote from a committee which carefully studies a number of statistics, including unemployment, sales, production, and shipments, as well as the real GNP.

When did large recessions occur?

In the fifty years since the outbreak of the great crash of 1929–1933, when more than one in five people lost their jobs and severe economic suffering was widespread, recessions have been identified as having occurred in 1938–1939, 1948–1949, 1953–1954, 1957–1958, 1960–1961, 1970–1971, 1974–1975, and another starting in 1980. The recessions of 1974–75 and the one beginning in 1980 both followed a *credit crunch* in which the growth of the money supply was dramatically reduced and unemployment rose quickly.

An examination of the dates shows that the postdepression recessions seem to be separated, from start to start, by anywhere from four to ten years. These recessions have been in evidence for at least a couple of centuries, with a separation of a little more than a decade being the most common phase. Since solar flares and sunspot activity follow a similar phase of just over a decade, some economists—most notably the nineteenth-century British economist, William Stanley Jevons—have linked the business and the sunspot cycles. The "theory" is that sunspots affect the weather and therefore crop yields and outputs. While even more direct claims have been made for the effects of sunspots on the economy, the decline in importance of agriculture in the overall economy has caused most economists to question the universality of Jevons's theory.

Are these the only cycles?

In economic charts the quite regular four-to-ten year fluctuations are sometimes superimposed onto much longer swings in economic conditions which span about fifty years from boom to boom or bust to bust. These longer swings are called *kondratieffs* after their Russian discoverer, who identified busts in the early 1800s, the 1840s, the 1890s, and the 1930s. There is no real theory for kondratieff cycles, which are primarily in the nature of historical observations. Some economists have identified the expansion phases with the development of major innovations—railroads in the recovery about 1850, automobiles in the post-1930s recovery, and so on. However, the root of these major swings still lies more in history than in theory, and their regularity is sufficient to leave some people feeling just a little uneasy as we move into the 1980s.

What should we do when we believe that a slump looms ahead?

Although we have made the point that it is difficult to ever know what economic conditions lie ahead, there are times when a majority feel that they do know. But what should we do to prepare ourselves for what looks like a slide? Here we see one of the most incredible findings that economic science has ever provided. We find that our individual inclinations and the nation's needs are absolutely and completely opposite. This remarkable conflict between desirable individual actions and those for the nation has become known as the *paradox of thrift*.

What is the paradox of thrift?

A great deal of credit for uncovering the paradox of thrift belongs to the economic genius of his time, John Maynard Keynes. He recognized that the conventional wisdom of many of his contemporaries ran directly counter to real needs. It was widely believed that if the economy were about to veer downward, we should prepare for it by building a savings cushion, which means, of course, spending less. Surely it would seem reasonable that if any individual were to be facing a reduction in income in the future, and he wished to remain in a position to make purchases, he should start saving now. As sound a policy as this is for an individual, it is the very opposite of the best action for the nation as a whole.

To save more of our incomes we must spend less. But this is the very characteristic of a demand-deficient economic recession. A recession means that demand is inadequate to keep everybody busy and on the job. The level of spending is too low. If a recession is about to occur, what is needed is more aggregate spending and not less. Yet the most prudent action for each individual is to save more and prepare for the bad times ahead.

Therein lies the paradox of thrift. What is a sensible policy for the individual is the worst policy for the aggregate. Individuals should be thrifty but the whole group should be making purchases. But it is not possible for all, as a whole, to spend more while each individual spends less. That is why Keynes argued that the government should step in and provide public spending. Sometimes the paradox of thrift is mentioned in the context of the classical fallacies of composition—cases where individual and aggregate effects are totally different.

Think for a moment of the effect if no official action is taken when the public anticipates hard times ahead. Members of the public will each separately want to save. By saving, they will not be buying goods and so people will lose their jobs. The very belief that times will be hard will make hard times. Even if the initial belief had been incorrect and a recession was not about to occur, the public's actions—based on their beliefs—will nevertheless make it occur. Expectations are self-fulfilling. If enough people believe in an impending slump, they will have their slump. That is why it is so important for government economists to always sound positive, even when every indication and every private economist points the other way. It is dangerous to let negative feelings spread, and if positive thinking and forecasting by the government can keep views optimistic, they'll give it a try. But can expectations be self-fulfilling the other way around? Can the expectation of inflation cause it to take place?

Can hyperinflation feed on itself?

At various times a popular notion has been that once inflation gets out of hand, the very fear of inflation can make it get worse. The argument runs like this:

If people think the prices of everything they want to buy will go up, they will not wait. Why wait until the price goes up when you can pay a lower price now? And so people buy, creating further demand, and prices will indeed go up. That just makes even more people believe that they should buy right away while they can afford what they want, and so the spiral is set in motion. So, at least, goes the panic-buying scenario that lies behind some people's view of the most frightening of all economic maladies—hyperinflation—when prices are on the gallop.

How bad can hyperinflation become?

Hyperinflation can indeed be bad. In parts of Europe earlier in the century, for example—especially in Germany in the early parts of the 1920s and in Hungary at virtually the same time—prices were doubling *every month*. With a doubling every month, prices would be 64 times (6400 percent) higher after a year. Keynes joked that Austrians bought two beers a time because they depreciated slower than money. (And you thought things were bad now?) If you ever collected postage stamps, you would have seen overstamping of millions and millions of German marks to mail a postcard. Before too long, at that rate, it would take a cartload of old money just to buy a newspaper. Things got so bad during the worst periods of the German and Hungarian hyperinflations that people were paid before lunch so that they could shop before prices had risen in the evening when they got off work. Barter became commonplace. This all makes South America's experience with inflation of just a couple of hundred percent a year look positively calm by comparison.

Can hyperinflation happen in America?

It is true that panic buying can feed on itself. Expectations of inflation can cause people to buy ahead and thereby cause prices to go up even more. But you can't pay a cartload of money for a newspaper unless the money has been printed up. Hyperinflation requires the complete and total help of the printing press. Without this, it must eventually fizzle out. In the past governments have printed excessive money when they have no other conventional means of collecting taxes; this might occur at the conclusion of a devastating war. We presumably have enough common sense to prevent this from ever happening in America. Otherwise, our only hope is that before things get too bad, we will run out of paper for printing more money.

With the two extremes of depression and hyperinflation, it would seem that there would be a happy medium in between, where we could enjoy full employment without inflation. That is what many economists used to think, at least before that rising problem of the late 1960s and the 1970s called stagflation.

What is stagflation?

Stagflation involves a stagnant economy with low growth in output and/or high unemployment, and yet, at the same time, a high rate of inflation. This, according to earlier Keynesian wisdom, should not occur. If we have high unemployment, the slack in the economy means low inflation. With low unemployment the pressure means high inflation. Otherwise, we are somewhere in between. This is the Phillips curve.

There is no doubt now that high unemployment and high inflation can exist at the same time. We have seen it happen over many years and in many different societies. We have also seen low growth and accompanying high inflation. If you don't think it has been witnessed in the United States—although the 1960s and 1970s show you to be wrong—take a look at Latin American. Many countries there have seen inflation of more than 100 percent per year, with unemployment simultaneously reaching into double digits.

What causes stagflation?

There are different ways to explain the cause of stagflation depending on what we mean. We could mean high unemployment with high inflation, or we could mean low growth in national output with high inflation. Both have been called stagflation, and yet the underlying causes are totally different. One is a short-run problem and the other is a long-term condition, one which we might have to live with for decades or centuries to come. So, let us discuss them in turn.

If, by stagflation, we mean high unemployment and high inflation, then this is the result of inflation working on the labor market. Suppose that inflation had been occurring for a lengthy spell because of excessive growth in the money supply. Let us repeat what we said about the monetarist view of unemployment. When prices have been rising for a long time, they become built into economic decisions that are made. In bargaining for wages, anticipated inflation for a given period will influence wage demands. If an employee would have settled for $10 and hour for the next two years if he thought prices would be stable, then he might well demand $12 an hour if he thinks that annual inflation will run at more than 10 percent.

Let us assume that the growth in the money supply is subsequently reduced. Actual inflation will begin to subside, perhaps falling back to 8 percent. The negotiated $12 an hour might now be too high a wage, and the supply of labor will exceed the demand. We will have rising unemployment as the demand for labor at $12 an hour falls short of the number wishing to work. Yet, at the same time, we will have 8 percent inflation, still a relatively high level.

We find that high unemployment and high inflation can go together at times when inflationary expectations have run ahead of actual events. But this is a short-run problem that will be corrected as people learn to adjust their inflationary expectations to the actual lower amount and bring their wage demands into line.

Is there a more serious cause of stagflation?

A more permanent, and therefore potentially more alarming, cause of stagflation appears when, by stagflation, we mean high inflation that is accompanied by stagnant real economic growth. And stagnant real economic growth, in the form of essentially unchanged living standards, doesn't necessarily mean a high level of unemployment. Living standards can be stagnant with everyone at work if the efficiency of the economy, judged by the progress of productivity, begins to wane. And such a decline in the growth of productivity has been registered in the United States over many years. Throughout the 1970s productivity has fallen in many sectors of the economy.

Our economy can provide us with a higher standard of living only if we put more factors of production into it. If we put more in we can get more out. The factors of production that we must inject are materials, human labor, and machines. These are then combined, using the technology that exists, in determining the size of the national output pie. We have been providing less of these factors of production; so runs the *real input/output* or *supply-side* macroeconomic view.

What is the new-wave supply-side view of economics?

Economists get caught up in fads, but every now and then they rediscover where they should really be going. Such an awakening came with the reevaluation of the importance of supply in the economy.

We have made it clear that the real objective of economic policy should be the national output, because that's what determines our living standard. This output requires inputs of the factors of production that we have just mentioned. That is, we require materials, people, and machines as well as the best technology. Only then can we show the high productivity that is necessary for a good economic standard of life. This means that economic policy—that which is aimed at raising output—should be geared to the inputs that create supply. These are not the policies that create aggregate demand, such as increasing money supply, government spending, and so on. Instead, they are policies such as tax credits to encourage businessmen to invest, income tax cuts to create an incentive to work, patent protection to provide an incentive to invent, and tax breaks for exploration, to encourage the discovery of minerals and fossil fuels.

Where are living standards going?

Recognition of the essential link between input and output in the economic production process makes it clear why our living standards have been declining. Because of shrinking natural resources and environmental protection, the input of raw materials cannot continue to grow at their former rapid rates, not unless space programs discover and provide untapped resource supplies. The input of labor, the second essential component of production, has also been constrained by the disincentive of high taxes needed to maintain our expanding social consciousness. This consciousness has been institutionalized within a multitude of official agencies. The *Laffer curve* of controversial economist Arthur Laffer links the reduced work incentive with this burden of tax. Laffer actually believes that lower tax rates would so raise the incentive to work—and hence income—that they could result in more taxes being collected. In addition, the programs that are financed from the taxes, such as unemployment, welfare, and the like, can reduce effort and willingness to work. This means that the payment of taxes and the programs financed by the taxes can both affect the input of labor.

The input of capital, which goes together with materials and labor in producing output, is also sadly in short supply. One possible explanation again flows from the environmental and social programs—which can be identified as a cause of reduced labor and material inputs. These programs require regulations to ensure their fulfillment. The regulations increase business risks and costs and cut incentives to invest in new plant and machinery.

Finally, the use of newer technologies, a leading route to continued growth in national output, has been checked by a healthy fear of their potential for inflicting environmental or bodily disasters. Restrictions on nuclear power plants and chemicals used in agriculture are just two of the more obvious examples of the limits placed on the adoption and development of new technology.

The pattern of growth in inputs gives the real supply-side view of the factors behind slow economic growth in material outputs. If there is slow growth in the input of raw materials, labor, and capital, and also in the development and adoption of improved technology, then ouput must also show slow growth. The accompanying inflation, which, together with slow growth, are the ingredients of the stagflation, can be the result of the slow growth itself. If government does not recognize slow growth for what it is—namely, the result of slowly growing inputs—it can easily be led to attempt to correct the situation by stimulating demand. But if the output is limited by the very real and binding physical constraints on the inputs, no demand policy can work, whether it is the monetary or the fiscal kind. This, some economists now believe, is the mistaken course of postwar demand-oriented policies—the belief that if only the aggregate demand is there, some magical process will produce the real supply. The attempt to achieve unreachable growth rates of output by stimulating demand—especially through a rising supply of money—explains why prices are in danger of being continually forced up. The slow or stagnant growth has in this way appeared concurrently with inflation—the two components of that funny word, but not so funny problem—stagflation.

Some people attempt to overcome stagnation in their own standard of living by dabbling in stocks and bonds. Let us explore these markets.

8

FINANCIAL MARKETS: STOCKS AND BONDS

October. This is one of the peculiary dangerous months to speculate in stocks in. The others are July, January, September, April, November, May, March, June, December, August, and February.

Mark Twain

There are two times in a man's life when he should not speculate: when he can't afford it and when he can.

Mark Twain

In what different ways can wealth be held?

A person's wealth can be held in many different forms. It can be put in real assets such as real estate, oil paintings, gold, soybeans, and antique furniture. These are not just real in the sense that they can be touched. They are also considered real in the way that GNP can be real; during inflation, their value should be unchanged in terms of the things their owners might choose to buy. Put differently, their current-dollar value should keep pace with inflation.

After real assets as a form of wealth come stocks, or corporate shares, and bonds. Stocks, or corporate shares, are just two names for the same thing. They are paper statements of ownership in the firms that issued them. As a part owner of the firm, the shareholder, or stockholder, is entitled to a share of the profit of the business. But before he is paid, any operating profits must be used to pay the holders of bonds.

Bondholders have merely made loans to the firm and do not own the business in any sort of way. The conditions on bonds require that all interest and repayments are met before any profit distribution can be made. Only after interest has been paid to the bondholder, and those with bonds that fall due are reimbursed, can shareholder profit—in the form of *dividends*—be paid. The part of the profit that is paid as dividends is determined after the firm has decided how much to retain for expansion. What is left after all this—the bondholder distributions and the retained earnings—is the amount available for the shareholders to enjoy. But even here, some must wait their turn. First to get a share of profit are the shareholders who are *preferred*. And even among these there is a ranking system. First paid are those who hold the shares that are *first* preferred. The *seconds* and others come later on. Only when the bondholders have been paid, when some profit has been retained, and the preferred stockholders have gotten their profit share can the poor old common shareholder hold out his hand. Common shareholders are the last in the lineup for profit distribution, but there are plenty who don't mind being called "common" when it comes to owning shares.

What asset is the least risky?

Because bondholders are paid first, they clearly have the lowest risk. The preferred stockholders come next and then the common stockholders. But even among the holders of the least risky class of financial assets—the bonds—there are a variety of risks. This can be judged by the rating of bonds.

The least risky are called AAA (triple A), and then come the AA (double A), and so on. These ratings are the result of assessments by those who make it their business to know, like the Moody and the Standard and Poor companies. The ratings are not unlike those on butter, eggs, and meat, except that the ratings are produced in the private sector.

Is money safer than bonds?

In terms of default risk, money is even safer than bonds. It is the most liquid component of financial wealth. However, it is the part on which earnings are lowest—frequently nothing, as it is on cash—which is why holding a lot of money is a likely sign of stupidity; the holder is foregoing the earnings that could be obtained on the alternative forms of wealth.

An alternative with very low risk is the short-term equivalent of bonds. These are called *bills* but, luckily, they are not things that the the holder has to pay. The holder of bills is always repaid within one year, but in all other respects a bill is just like a bond. The United States Treasury is the largest issuer of bills and bonds, which are required to finance the deficit between government spending and taxes. The bills trade in the so-called money market, and bonds trade in the capital market.

What is the value of a bond?

Bonds come in two major varieties—in *discount* form or as a *coupon* (clippable) bond. A discount bond might offer the holder $100 at the end of one year after he had bought it at the beginning of that year for $95, a "discount" of 5 percent. By paying $95 and getting $100 after one year, the bond-holder would enjoy approximately a 5 percent return.

A coupon bond promises the holder a regular income stream. By paying a total of $100 for the bond, the holder might be promised $5 at the end of each year for a number of years, with his $100 back at some later specified time. These are the types of bonds that we shall consider in determining the value of a bond. We might begin by asking how much somebody would pay now for a promised income stream of $5 a year for a long time.

What is the value of a permanent $5 a year?

Let us consider a bond on which the risks of nonpayment are absolutely minimal or even zero. This "riskless" bond could be one issued by the U.S. government, on which repayment is limited only by the ability of the government to collect money for its interest payments by taxing us all. Now let us ask this: How much would you pay the U.S. government for its bond that promises you and your successors and whoever owns the bond $5 each and every year forever and ever? Although the U.S. government does not appear to enjoy issuing such bonds, there are other governments and other institutions that have issued these *perpetual* bonds, which are known in some quarters as *consols*.

The amount that you would be willing to pay for a five-dollar-per-year income stream, if you think that annual interest rates will forever be about 5 percent on ordinary finite-length bonds, will be $100. How do we arrive at this? Well, if you believed that each year you would be able to earn 5 percent on one-, two-, or five-year bonds, you could take $100 and get $5 a year. And when the finite bond matured, even if you had spent your interest, you could reinvest your $100. Because of this alternative option, you would not want to pay more than $100 for the infinite $5 stream; if you did, your bond yield is less than from the continuous stream available on a succession of the alternative finite-length bonds.

What would happen if the interest rate rose to 10 percent?

Suppose that the interest rates on newly issued bonds were to rise to 10 percent a year and that people expected them to remain at this higher level. How much would people then pay for the bond that promises $5 coupons for an infinite number of years? The answer is that they would pay only $50. They would be silly to pay more than this when the $50 worth of new bonds at 10 percent would still give them $5 a year. And that, for those who didn't know, is why bond prices fall when interest rates rise.

Can we directly compute market values of perpetuals?

We illustrated how a security value is determined with a perpetual type of bond. We learn that a steady and riskless $5 income stream, when interest rates are 5 percent, is worth $100. This is $5 divided by the interest rate in decimal form, or 0.05. When interest rates rise to 10 percent, the value of the $5 income stream falls to only $50, which is again $5 divided by the higher interest rate in decimal form, or 0.1. In general, the market value of a perpetual bond is discovered by dividing the coupon by the interest rate.

The most familiar form of income is that which is earned by human beings. Because income is earned by people just as on bonds, we can think of the value of *human wealth* by applying the principle for valuing a bond.

What is the value of human wealth?

As a graduate student, I was once asked the expected dollar value of myself—a human being who was training to become a professor of economics. I quickly calculated that a $50,000 per year income was the absolute top, and assuming an interest rate of 5 percent and many, many years at this high income, I arrived at the value of $1 million (or $50,000 divided by the interest rate of 0.05). The solution takes advantage of the large number of years, making the problem like that of valuing a perpetual bond. "No you are not," I was told. "You are worth $1.97." This was the value of the chemical ingredients of the human body, which contained, then as now, so much calcium at so much an ounce, so much iron at so much an ounce, and so on; water was calculated as being free.

Of course, the approximate value of the chemical ingredients of the human body, even allowing for inflation, *is* only a couple of dollars. However, the important feature of the human body, to whomever it belongs, is *the way the chemical components are combined*—a way that results in a human being such as you or I. Because the chemicals are so perfectly combined, the value of the human being exceeds the value of the parts. Human wealth should be valued like a bond, at so many millions of dollars for an economist, rather than by adding the costs of the separate chemical ingredients. (Of course, the full value of a human can never be calculated, especially when we try to value ourselves.) Human wealth, and how people separately attempt to maximize their own wealth by deciding, for example, on how much education to undertake, is a branch of economic study often called *human capital theory*.

What does this mean for computing national wealth?

It should now be clear that the value of all the machines, factories, roads, buildings, and other physical things is only a part of the wealth of any nation. We should also include wealth of the human kind. Moreover, total value depends on the efficient or effective combination of components in the national economy. A sensible way of finding the purely economic value of the wealth of an economy is to treat it like a bond, that is, take the national yearly income and divide it by the rate of interest. This interest rate is hard to select because it should depend on prospects for growth, risk, and the like, but the procedure is at least as smart as trying to add up separate parts and calling it the national wealth while leaving aside human beings and the efficiency with which resources are combined.

Since it is difficult to compute the national wealth, we might wonder whether its value moves up and down with the stock market, which is, after all, where lots of wealth changes hands. What everybody wants answered is:

What makes the stock market go up and down?

Obviously, if we knew what makes the stock market do what it does, we wouldn't have to write books and teach economics. So that means I don't have the answer. No one, including myself, knows what makes the stock market rise and decline. Some people believe it moves with women's hemlines—down in the 1930s, up in the 1960s with miniskirts; and they're not sure where it's going in the 1980s. Other people subscribe to relationships between football games and stock indexes. (Someone observed that when original NFL teams prove victorious in superbowl games, stock indexes tend to rise over the following months.) Clearly and more seriously, if any person, by some fantastic skill, did solve the mystery of market ups and downs, that person would not be very likely to reveal what he knew.

Despite these obvious truths, we still often rely on so-called professional advice. The truth of the matter is that no one knows why stock prices go up and down because stock markets are *efficient*.

What is market efficiency?

By efficiency, we can mean a lot of things. Most immediately, we mean that everything that can possibly be known is considered and included in the prices we see. If it is known that great profits lie ahead for the international airlines, then the current price of these stocks will already be appropriately high. This should straightaway suggest a second meaning of efficiency—there are no bargains to be had, nor are there any definite "dogs." If all good information, as well as the bad, is already included and reflected in the price of the stock, then higher prices must be paid for the better stocks. But isn't that always the way it is? There's no surefire and easy way to get rich in the stock market.

Stock-market efficiency can be viewed in still another way. If forces were such that the price of a stock were sure to rise the next day—or month or year—by a large amount, what would you do? You would act on this belief and buy the stock now in the hope of reaping the future gains. But if everybody knows what you know, your knowledge will do you no good. Others who might sell you the stock will be demanding a high price because they have the same information you do. The price of the stock will not rise the next day. It will already be high. So, what is a poor investor going to do? Maybe he should leave things alone and take a casual and relaxing *random walk*.

What is a random walk?

A random walk is the immediate result of market efficiency. If everything there is to be known is already reflected in the stock's price, then such information is of no consequence. Only new items of news should have an effect, and since the new news is as likely to be good as bad, an increase in any stock price is just as likely as a decline. Therefore, if your next step were as likely to be in one direction as in another, you would be taking a random stroll. That is the nature of a random walk: With prices as likely to move up as down, the progress of the price of stocks would chart an irregular pattern. It's as simple and as rational as that. The pattern is studied with magnificent math by Ph.D.-qualified experts in the better university business schools, such as the University of Chicago, MIT, Berkeley, and British Columbia in Canada. But the essence of the concept could be learned as early as the age at which we learn to walk straight, or almost.

Why, then, all the professional advice?

Why, indeed? If professionals cannot point to any bargains or certain bets, then they can hardly pay their way. And efficiency ensures that this must be the case. It's hard to explain why anyone would pay to add nothing to their odds of success. But maybe markets become efficient only because the professionals have discovered bargains, bidding their prices to where they should be, or maybe the professionals know something we don't, simply by working on the inside?

Is there an advantage to inside information?

You bet there is, which is why its use is illegal and why potential abuse is watched like a hawk by the Securities and Exchange Commission (SEC). It is apparent from our discussion of efficiency that if all available information is already reflected in the price, then the only type of information to have is that which is available to no one else. Then, if the news is good, you can buy the stock without the seller extracting the true value or price. Inside information about abnormally high profit would be of great help, and it is possible that people believe they can buy this. There is probably a return from time and money spent gathering information, but no one is likely to sell it, since after one sale, it becomes a public good and it's then hard to profit from further sales.

How can we do well on the stock market, legally?

The fabulously successful investor, Lord John Maynard Keynes, knew that to make money you do not need to know the intrinsic value of stock. Rather, all the successful investor requires is a sound judgment of the thinking of *others* about what the stock *should* be doing. If others believe that stock prices should rise, whatever the validity of their belief, then prices will rise and it would be a good idea to buy. The belief of others in general, when acted upon, will be the force behind the market, and the good judge of market psychology will sense that force and profit from it.

Keynes illustrated his uncanny feeling for the stock market by referring to a favorite British newspaper game. The less-serious daily papers and the gossipy Sunday rags have not infrequently published collections of pictures of beautiful girls. The task of the reader is to rank the pictures in the collection according to their beauty. The winner is the one whose ranking comes closest to that of a "panel of experts."

What is required to win this questionable "quiz"? It is not the possession of good judgment about beautiful girls. Instead, the skill needed is the ability to correctly anticipate the order in which the panel of judges will place the girls. A good eye for pretty girls will not do. A good judgment of others' judgments of girls is what is required. And so goes the market for stocks, where future values are as subjective as enduring beauty.

Bulls and bears—a visit to the zoo?

I don't know why it ever came out this way, but when things went well, someone must have thought it was a lot of bull. Seriously, though, a *bull market* is a healthy one that charges ahead, and a *bear market* wants to lie down.

Is there a lot of market bull?

Bull is very cheap because there is a mountainous supply. Here is a choice bit of bull: "The stock market rose today with buyers greatly outnumbering sellers." But this cannot be true. It is impossible for the number of buyers to exceed the number of sellers by even one. How can you be a buyer unless someone made the sale? The number of shares bought and the numbers sold must be absolutely the same. A buy and a sell are just two sides of the same transaction and, like every apple, there are two sides—an inside and an outside— or, in our case, a buyer and a seller.

Then how about this? "Stocks closed slightly lower today, with profit-taking after a week of steady gains." "Profit-taking?" This is another way of saying: "We do not know what went on here today." What kind of foolish investor would cash in a stock if its price had managed to rise and he thought it would make further gains. It's as foolish to sell stock because its price goes up as it is to buy stock because its price goes down. And you don't hear the analysts calling the latter "profit-giving." But if profit-taking means taking from someone else, then who is the someone else who is foolishly giving on the other side? No, if you buy the term profit-taking, you are being taken for a ride.

What strategies do make sense in the stock market?

No buying or selling strategy can possibly make you rich, which should be clear from understanding efficiency or the consequence of efficiency—namely, the random walk. There are, however, things you can do to reduce risks, and care in avoiding risks can be of great value.

There are mountains of financial theories and computer-produced evidence which suggest that putting all your eggs in one basket means taking a big chance. Well, without the mass of expensive theories and evidence, the conclusion should hardly be difficult to swallow. Eggs and baskets, and clichés made from them, have been around a long time. A good portfolio of stocks and bonds is one that is well diversified. This means that it contains a variety of stocks which will reduce the risks because some things can go up while others go down, and it should all average out.

What if we only have a rather small pot of wealth?

For those with a small amount to invest there is the mutual fund. If we are unable to individually own diversified holdings, we can at least share in them with others. A mutual fund will buy a portfolio of stocks and bonds in large amounts. It then offers shares of these diversified holdings to the public at large. That way, with a modest amount of funds, we may buy ourselves a nicely diversified portfolio.

Are all mutual funds the same?

The mutual funds, like all of us, find it useful to specialize. Some offer funds that look good in pension plans, and others offer funds that look like they could fly or crash. They differ in the amount that they cost to run and in the performance they finally produce, so it pays to shop around. Most funds and stocks in general do poorly in inflation.

Why haven't stock prices kept pace with inflation?

During the 1970s, when the price level almost doubled, the stock market, as reflected in the much-quoted Dow Jones Industrial Index, actually fell. Even if the stock market had risen—but by less than prices in general—we would have reason to be puzzled.

If inflation raises prices and production costs by the same percentage, then the difference between these—that is, profits—should also rise by the same percentage. For example, if, before inflation, a firm sold jeans at $20 a pair and they cost $15 a pair to produce, it would have made a profit of $5 a pair. If inflation raises prices and costs by 20 percent—to $24 and $18, respectively—the profits, or the difference, rise to $6 a pair. This means that profits rise by 20 percent—from $5 to $6 a pair—which keeps profits in line with inflation. Since stocks are the claims on profits, why haven't stock prices risen by as much as inflation in general? This example and just plain old common sense should suggest that they would.

The fact that stock prices have not only failed to keep pace with inflation, but have actually declined, is one of the mysteries of the 1970s. We do know that the *profits* of the companies whose shares trade in the stock market have, at least to a degree, kept pace with inflation. But *stock prices* have not. With dividends rising along with profits, but stock prices not going up, the return on stock that is given by dividends as a percent of market value of stock has increased. Higher risks that cannot be avoided or diversified by stock buyers could explain part of the higher return as a compensation for this risk, but the rest remains a mystery.

Unfortunately, economics cannot explain everything, and the stock market has proved difficult when it comes to explaining the effects of the inflation of the 1970s. If stock prices are difficult to explain, how about bonds?

How do bond markets behave?

We have explored the value of bonds earlier in this chapter and have seen how they rise when interest rates are on the decline. But what makes interest rates go up and down?

Interest rates are the payments that must be made for borrowing money. If you increase the supply of money available to be lent, the price of borrowing money—the interest rate—will come down, and depressed interest rates raise the price of bonds. If the demand for funds happens to increase because people have all sorts of spending plans, the price of borrowing the funds will rise. This will reduce bond prices.

But this is only a part of the forces that lie behind the interest rate and the price of bonds. Nearly a century ago, an outstanding American economist named Irving Fisher (not related to the very fine twentieth-century MIT economist, Stanley, who spells his name Fischer) realized that lenders worried about inflation. Fisher argued, with great force, that when inflation was expected to be high, those who provided funds to be lent would demand compensation. If interest rates were 4 percent without inflation, then to keep pace with the price of goods when inflation was anticipated at 8 percent, the interest rate would move to 12 percent. This would depress the price of bonds. We discussed this point much earlier but did not give it a name. The phenomenon has become known as the *Fisher effect*. Tests of interest-rate movements during inflation show that Fisher's hypothesis is at least substantially correct, and that expected inflation has therefore played a major part in pricing bonds.

Do taxes play a role?

When we said that if interest rates were 4 percent with no inflation, then they would be 12 percent with anticipated inflation of 8 percent, we failed to include taxes. In actual fact interest earnings do tend to be taxed as part of your income. Your 4 percent interest with no inflation, and with, for example, a 50 percent marginal personal income-tax rate, gives just 2 percent return after taxes. Even if you did receive 12 percent interest because you expected 8 percent inflation, if you paid 50 percent in taxes, you'd actually earn—after taxes—only 6 percent; you'd lose 2 percent of buying power.

With an 8-percent rate of inflation, we need interest rates of 20 percent to maintain earnings of 2 percent after inflation and taxes. This will give 10 percent after taxes, which, with 8 percent going toward inflation, is 2 percent of "real" return. Isn't that absolutely incredible! An 8-percent expected inflation would have to produce a 20-percent interest rate to leave people as well off as before.

Don't think that borrowers won't borrow at these rates. Interest payments by borrowers can be deducted against income before paying taxes. This means that if borrowers also have a 50 percent taxation rate, 20 percent interest rates after 50 percent of interest payments have been used to reduce taxes are only 10 percent after taxes. Since, with 8 percent inflation, what is purchased with the borrowed money will, on average, increase in value by 8 percent, the real interest paid at a 20-percent rate is only 2 percent. It isn't done with mirrors. Taxes require interest rates to rise by more than inflation to compensate lenders. Borrowers are prepared to pay. However, compensation is only partial. According to historical evidence, savers lose after taxes.

Are all interest rates alike?

We often talk as if there were only one rate, but in actual fact there are numerous rates of interest that vary according to the risk of the bond, with the riskier bonds offering a higher amount in order to compensate for that risk. Interest rates also vary with the maturity of the loan and sometimes even with the amount.

What is the discount rate?

The discount rate is the rate charged by the Federal Reserve System on loans to commercial banks. Indeed, it was mentioned when we explained how the Fed affects the supply of money. The Fed is the *lender of last resort*. This means that if a bank does not have sufficient reserves to meet its reserve requirements, it can borrow them at a penalty interest rate from the Federal Reserve.

The discount rate is changed only infrequently, when the Fed wishes to influence the money supply by changing the number of banks showing up at its so-called discount window to borrow extra reserves. The highest rate ever reached was 16 percent, which was charged to heavy borrower banks during a brief interval in the spring of 1980, and again in the fall of 1980 and the beginning of 1981.

Is the prime interest rate the most important?

The prime rate of interest is the rate of interest that banks charge their very best corporate clients. Rates on loans to most others are set by adding to the prime rate.

Before we leave the topic of interest rates and the factors that determine the prices of stocks and bonds, we should admit that there are many questions we have not asked and which economists cannot answer. Believe it or not, many economists never study the topic of personal finance and have trouble balancing their bank accounts.

What do economists know about bookkeeping and personal finance?

An economist is just as likely as anybody else to have a lot of month left at the end of his money. You will perhaps recall that the only accounts that attract the economists' interest are the national income and the balance of payments. Economists do not discuss bookkeeping and individuals' accounts. This is left to the experts—the accountants—and plenty of economics Ph.D.s are permanently perplexed by what income tax forms require and how to have money at the end of the month. Economists study economics, not economy.

Economists not only know little about bookkeeping and personal finance, but they frequently know little of the jargon used by the accountants and stockbrokers who do specialize in these things. But economists do know how much the jargon is worth.

How important is financial jargon?

There are many highly technical, fancy terms that are used to describe special financial instruments in the stock and bond markets. There are extendibles and retractibles, detachables and convertibles, and even more virtually incomprehensibles. But knowledge of the finer details of actual financial affairs are best left to those who need to know these things to make their living. To the majority of people, this high finance and business accounting is dreadfully dull, and that's why relatively few spend their time at it. This supply shortage of those able and willing to work as accountants and as stockbrokers raises their price—that is, their salary. On the other hand, because of the extra fun and joy in economics, there is a high supply of university professors of economics, even though the training is long and it's essential to be very clever. This high supply of willing economics professors keeps down their pecuniary rewards—that is, their wages. But the nonpecuniary reward, the fun of the subject, is still theirs.

With all this use of supply and demand, we should make sure we're using it correctly. Supply and demand is the central tool used in the very revealing theories of the consumer and the firm.

III

The Economics of Consumers and Firms

9

LAWS OF SUPPLY
AND DEMAND

*The whole civilized world is now eager to know whether in the future
the high cost of living is to advance further, recede, or remain station-
ary. Even the best forecasts I have seen appear to be based on a very
incomplete comprehension of the problem. Many conceive it as a
problem of ordinary supply and demand and discuss the general price
level as they would discuss the price of wheat or any other commodity, overlooking the fact that causes affecting price levels are as distinct from those affecting an individual price as the causes affecting
the tides are distinct from those affecting an individual wave.*

Irving Fisher (1912)

Why do individual prices change?

We have learned that the rate at which prices in general
are changing is the rate of inflation, and that prices in general are measured by some sort of price index. We have also
learned what lies behind inflation in terms of the money
supply and other macroeconomic influences.

When it comes to a discussion of individual prices, the
economist—in this case, the microeconomist—changes his
approach and uses the law of supply and demand that we
are about to present. You might well wonder why the economist explains prices in general in one way—for example,
using the money supply—and individual prices in another

way—using supply and demand. Well, you're in good company. A large number of very famous economists have also wondered, often critically and out loud. But that hasn't stopped them from continuing to use a different bag of tools in tackling macroeconomic problems than the bag used in microeconomics.

One way they try to get around this suspicious practice is to talk about inflation as an *absolute price problem* and individual prices as a *relative price problem*. Supply and demand is the method reserved for showing why some prices—relative prices—move more or less than others.

Distinguishing between absolute and relative prices isn't a completely satisfactory excuse for what is done. In truth, many economists would agree that microeconomics, captured in supply and demand, is the real foundation of all of economics. If some integration of micro- and macroeconomic theories is in order, it is the microeconomics that should be extended into macroeconomics, and not the reverse. When this is done, inflation becomes the result of raising the supply of money above the demand for money. This will reduce the value of money, which is the same as saying that it takes more of it to purchase the things we want. This is nothing other than inflation. Thus, the same supply and demand rule applies to individual prices as to prices in general, or inflation.

Why should we distinguish between price levels and individual prices?

If we believed—or even knew—that inflation next year, for example, would run at 10 percent, this would not tell us what would happen to the price of cheese or home heating oil. Yet, if we were dairy farmers, oil company executives, or people who like to eat or keep warm, we might care very much about these particular prices. It is true that individual consumers and firms are all part of the economy and will, *on average*, experience the booms and busts that the entire economy goes through. But most of us are not just "average" and, instead, happen to work in this or that particular business and buy particular types of goods. The firms that produce the cheese or oil would like to know what will happen to the prices of what they sell. The consumer living in the north will care about the price of heating oil, and the lover of good cheese will care about how much he or she must pay to indulge his or her pleasure.

Microeconomics is concerned with individuals' pleasures and sacrifices. It tells businesses how best to survive competition and consumers how to survive the forces of supply and demand that shape their working lives and the prices of what they need to buy.

What is the law of supply and demand?

It is usual to express the law of supply and demand in terms of *curves* or *schedules*. However, many humans are more confortable with words than with mathematics or geometry, and there is no reason why these people cannot learn to understand and work with the law of supply and demand. The law is straightforward and makes such good common sense that we can be at home with it in no time. Let's start out with supply and then deal with demand. We can begin by proving that businessmen will want to send more to market or, in other words, increase supply, when the prices at which they can sell their wares are high. Obvious? Of course it is, but we should show why it is true, because it turns out to depend on the *law of diminishing returns*.

What is the law of diminishing returns?

Diminishing returns will eventually set into almost any-thing, although it is hoped that it has not yet affected the de-gree of knowledge and enjoyment you are obtaining through learning about economics. The law of diminishing returns is generally explained by referring to events on the farm, and although few of you—and few economists—have much practical knowledge of farming, the example should convince you.

Imagine a farmer working a small plot of land. If he were joined by a hired hand on that same plot of land, the two pairs of hands would surely produce more. The output of the plot might double, or perhaps increase by even more. But say a third man came to help, and a fourth, and a fifth and so on. It would be only a matter of time before an extra man adds less to production than was added by the man who came before. Let us clarify this. We are not saying that he *lowers* the output of the plot of land, but only that additional help will eventually *add less* extra output, because we al-ready have more farmers working on this same small plot of land. If you still need convincing, imagine the one-hun-dredth farmer added to help in the production of potatoes on a tiny square of land.

This is the law of diminishing returns. As we add addi-tional factors of production—in this case, labor—to augment output when another factor of production is constrained—in this case, land—an additional unit of the variable factor will add less output than the unit before. Expressed differently, as we try to get steadily more output from a given plot of land, the cost of that extra output will become more and more. This is the law of diminishing returns. It applies to factories with a given plant size just as much as it does to farm produce. It is because costs increase as we try to produce more that there is a limit on what firms like to supply. Let us show this by using some numbers, and ask:

How do rising costs limit output?

Suppose a product can be sold at $10 a unit and the cost of producing it starts at $8. There's a $2 profit for each item that the firm supplies. So why ever stop supplying the product if there's $2 more profit from each extra unit that is produced; the more items produced, the bigger the profit. Obviously what the firm will then supply is limited only by demand. But, for *one individual or firm,* the total market demand could be viewed as unlimited.

A producer will want to continue to add to the supply as long as production costs remain less than $10 per unit. However, when increasing output along the path of diminishing returns causes production costs to rise above $10 per unit, losses are incurred by making more. Clearly, if we can sell our wares at $10 each and they cost more than this to manufacture, we'll be losing money on those items that we make. This gives us the rule of how much to supply.

When we can sell our produce for more than the production costs, we continue to add to the supply. As unit production costs rise because of increased production, to the point of equaling the selling price, we stop at that production level. With costs rising from diminishing returns, we should produce until unit costs reach the market price. We learn that the last item produced will have a production cost just about equal to the selling price. So, if we call the cost of one extra unit of output the *marginal cost,* the firm should raise production until the marginal cost equals the selling price.

If, for some reason, the selling price the firm receives for its product happens to go up, at the existing output profits will be made on the last item produced. It then pays to produce and supply more at the higher price, and production should rise until the unit costs, increasing along the path of diminishing returns, equals the higher market price. Similarly, if the market price the firm receives were to fall, costs would exceed the reduced price at the existing output levels. Only if output and supply falls will costs decline until they again equal the lower market price. This is the *law of supply:* Firms supply more at higher market prices. So now what about the law of demand? Just as the law of supply comes from diminishing returns, the law of demand comes from *opportunity costs.*

What does an opportunity cost?

Opportunity costs are the truly relevant costs. When you buy a shirt or a meal for $20, that is the actual amount paid. But what must you give up? It makes you give up, or forgo, $20 of what you would like to spend on something else, such as some jeans or an economics book. Opportunity costs are not limited to individuals' choices. When a local government decides on a new hospital, it may have to give up a new building for a school; or when the national government spends more on defense, it will have less for social programs. What is given up is the opportunity cost, just as in our discussion of money demand the opportunity cost of currency or interest-free checking accounts is the alternative interest that's forgone.

Opportunity costs exist because our incomes are limited or because things are scarce. We therefore have to make choices, and it is the theory of these choices that is the *law of demand*.

What is the law of demand?

As the market price rises on any individual item we buy, we must give up more of something else, and as individual prices fall, we give up less. Higher prices mean a greater opportunity cost, and that greater cost determines what we want to buy. This is the law of demand: Consumers demand less at higher market prices and more at lower market prices. This is quite obvious, but remember that it is because of opportunity cost. There is also an effect of higher prices on our real income but we consider the *income effect* as a separate factor.

The fact that we must give up more at higher prices and give up less at lower prices gives the effect of prices on an individual's demand. Higher beef prices—and other prices unchanged—will cause each individual to buy less beef and more chicken or lamb. But if this is true of each indivdual, or even with most of them, it must also be true of everyone taken as a whole. Higher prices for goods or services make consumers as a group demand less, and lower prices make them demand more. Writing this law of demand side by side with the law of supply we have:

The law of supply: Firms supply more at higher market prices and less at lower market prices.

The law of demand: Consumers demand less at higher market prices and more at lower market prices.

We will soon be ready to apply the law of supply and demand to some interesting problems, but first we should show how supply and demand determine prices.

How do supply and demand determine market prices?

The law of supply tells us how much firms will want to sell at different market prices, and the law of demand tells us how much consumers will want to buy at these prices. But when taken separately, neither law can tell us what prices themselves will be. However, when we put the law of supply and the law of demand together, we have the law of supply and demand that gives us market prices. According to the law of supply and demand, the price of any product will be where the supply and demand for that product are equal. The easiest way to prove that this will happen is to start out with supply equal to demand and then ask what would happen if the market price were to change so that supply and demand were no longer equal. What would happen?

The law of supply says that as prices go up, firms would like to produce and supply more. On the other hand, the law of demand says that as prices go up, consumers would like to buy less. If we had started out with a price where firms were supplying an amount equal to what consumers were buying, the presumed increase in price would create a glut on the market. The shelves and the warehouses where the product was stored would begin to fill up as production continued to run ahead of what was purchased. If the product were perishable—such as butter or eggs—there would be immediate pressure to cut the price in order to sell off the excess. But even if the product could be stored, there are costs involved from unsold output, including tied-up funds. Again, there are pressures to cut prices, perhaps by running a sale. We find that if the price goes above the level where supply equals demand, there are price-cutting pressures on the producer, who wishes to avoid having a surplus of unsold output.

What happens if price falls?

Now let us see what would happen if, instead of a price rising after having been at the point where supply equals demand, the price were to fall. At the lower price, the quantity that firms would want to produce would go down according to the law of supply. On the other hand, the quantity that consumers would want to buy would rise. With less being produced and more being demanded, there would be a shortage. Those consumers who were unable to find what they wanted might offer a little more for a product if it would ensure their supply. Alternatively, with the shortage, producers would realize that they could raise prices and still be able to sell all that they make. We discover that pressure from the buyers to get what they want, or taking advantage of opportunities by the sellers, would push up prices that had fallen after being at the point where supply equals demand.

We now have the law of supply and demand: The price will tend toward the point where supply equals demand. If the price is higher than that, there is a surplus. This will bring the price down. If the price is lower than that, there will be a shortage. This will bring the price up. The only place where the price can remain, *if all other things are equal,* is the point where supply equals demand. We call this the *equilibrium price,* because this is the only *balance* price. If the price were elsewhere, it would move toward the level of equality of supply and demand.

Does supply ever increase as prices go down?

The law of supply argues that firms will wish to produce more as market prices go up and less as prices come down. But what if unit costs decline as a firm adds to output? Or, in other words, what if the law of diminishing returns does not hold? Then, if the market price remains stable, the more the firm produces, the larger the profit it makes as unit costs decline. This would violate a law of supply that is based on diminishing returns, but, as we shall show, a violation is unlikely once we distinguish between returns-to-scale and diminishing returns.

What are returns–to–scale?

If there is no quantity limitation on any factor of production we will not have diminishing returns. The law of diminishing returns applies only where production is constrained by size limitations, of the farm or the factory floor, for example. When we can vary all factors of production together, we have the case of *"returns-to-scale."*

Unlike the case where one factor is constrained, we do not know in which direction there will be returns-to-scale. When more farmers work with more land, there is no reason to think that the output of an extra farmer on an extra piece of land will decline. Indeed, if farmers can get together and help each other—perhaps by jointly buying an expensive piece of farm equipment that it would not pay to own separately—the output of each farmer could actually rise, as there are more farmers and more land. In such a case, we say that there are *increasing* returns-to-scale. The word *scale* is used because we are changing the quantity of *all* the factors of production that are involved. There are, for example, increasing returns-to-scale in the production of electronic calculators and television sets. This is because longer production runs allow more capital equipment to be used which lowers unit costs. If costs per unit rise, even when all factors of production are applied in larger amounts, we say that there are *diminishing* returns-to-scale, and if unit costs remain unchanged, we talk of *constant returns*.

What is important to the law of supply is the law of diminishing returns and *not* the returns-to-scale. Every firm and every farm, at a given point in time, must accept its existing size. It is not possible to instantly add to the size of the plant or farm. These things take some time. Buildings must be erected and land acquired and prepared. And while the plant or farm is fixed in size, diminishing returns will eventually and invariably occur. Given a longer span of time, circumstances might well change when market conditions allow. But the law of supply that we have used refers to the best output of the firm at different prices while it is at a relatively fixed size. The law of supply is not violated in the short run by returns-to-scale, although eventually, as plant size is changed, we should consider what it means. We will leave this problem until we discuss the questions that are raised by natural monopolies.

Diminishing returns might well always guarantee the law of supply, but can we be so sure about demand? In particular:

Does demand ever increase as prices go up?

There are some unusual cases where the law of demand is violated and where higher prices may actually cause some people to buy more. These cases, however, are very rare and don't give sufficient reason to reject our law. They occur when buyers judge the quality of an article by its price. Let us take an example.

I have a friend who was once selling oil paintings from Taiwan. They were mass produced, even though they were painted by hand, and each artist made trivial variations on a theme. It was often difficult to tell two paintings apart. The Taiwanese artists took fabulously authentic sounding Western names like Gianini, VanDusen, Pascal, and Scott.

My friend first tried a 100 percent markup and priced the paintings, including frames, at $12 each. They didn't sell, and he was finally forced by a financial bind to unload his entire stock to someone else, who tried a new tack. Gianini's were put up for sale at $100 each. Scott's and Pascal's were priced at $150, and even for small VanDusen's he asked $200. All of the paintings were quickly sold.

We often judge an item by its price if we know little else about it. What happened here is that people did just that. When items are as difficult to judge as art, our perception of what we are buying is influenced by the price. Some cheaper jewelry might face a similar situation of demand. "If the price is $5, it must be junk, but this one at $25 is probably O.K." But it's hard to think of many cases where this might occur and where sales would increase at a higher price. We could even be semantic and claim that the product in the buyer's mind is different and changes as the price goes up, and that greater enjoyment or satisfaction is gained from more expensive paintings and jewelry, even if the more expensive items are not necessarily of higher quality. Alternatively, we can say that the buyer believes he or she finds information about the quality of the product in the price that is charged. Quite often this is a readily available and accurate way of gaining information on quality, because, in general, better items do cost more. However, most items that a consumer buys can be evaluated by means other than price, and these "violations" of the law of demand will therefore be very rare—if we even consider them as being violations rather than just special cases of demand.

If violations in the separate laws of supply and demand are unlikely, then how about violations in the one law of supply and demand, which is the law where we combine supply and demand to determine market price?

Do we ever find violations of the law of supply and demand?

The plain answer is that when there is no major market intervention by the government or a trade union, and there is no other type of restrictive practice, prices are invariably at the point where supply equals demand, except during temporary adjustments to changed circumstances. And even when there is government intervention or some restrictive practice, supply is generally equal to demand if we carefully include everything in the supply and demand, or if we include all elements within the price that is paid.

This doesn't mean that there aren't moments when there is a temporary difference between supply and demand. We know, for example, that if prices fall short of where supply and demand are equal, people will demand more than producers are prepared to supply, which causes consumers to be prepared to offer more and producers to begin to charge more. But it might take a little while before producers get around to putting on the higher-price stickers, and it might not be expedient to charge more to good customers until all the competitors have raised their prices. In the meantime, supply might not equal demand, but "meantime" is of short duration. The only price at which we are in balance or equilibrium is where supply equals demand, and this price will be quickly found, if there is no interference.

There are some prices that the government has tried to keep below where they should be and others that it has tried to keep above their free-market levels. Rent controls and price regulations on oil and natural gas are examples of prices that have been kept artificially low, and agricultural price supports and minimum-wage laws are examples of prices that have been kept artificially high. While wisdom seems to have reached the government with a wave of energy price deregulations and a limited removal of agricultural price supports, we still live with rent control in many cities, specific government grain-purchase programs, minimum-wage laws, interest-rate ceilings on savings deposits and loans in some states, and so on. A couple of these are well worth examining.

What do rent controls do to the law of supply and demand?

Rent controls mean that tenants gain and landlords lose. If the intent of the controls is to redistribute wealth, then they succeed. However, at the artificially low rents, there is a greater demand for rent controlled housing, as people prefer it to uncontrolled housing. This is the conclusion of the law of demand—lower prices mean more demand. At the low rents on the controlled housing, there is little incentive to build more. Growth in supply is reduced. There is even an incentive to allow existing housing to deteriorate if, as is the case in many American cities, newer housing is uncontrolled. Thus, controlled housing can become slum housing. The housing supply is reduced. Allowing limited rent increases on controlled housing will modify but not eliminate these effects.

As rent controls create housing shortages, those people

who would like to have controlled rents will offer *key money* as bribes. These extra payments make the total payments more in line with what will clear the market. Rent controls are not the only example of price control creating shortages. An additional example is controls on interest rates.

What do interest controls do?

In an effort to provide financial institutions with a cheap source of funds so that they could advance cheap mortgages to home buyers, there have been interest-rate ceilings on what the institutions can pay to their depositors. This means, however, that when market interest rates are high, the financial institutions could be restricted in paying sufficient interest to attract funds from unregulated parts of the financial markets.

The move designed to make cheap mortages available means there would be no mortgages. The demand for funds from the savings and loan and thrift institutions exceeds the available supply. To overcome this, they offer noninterest "returns," such as electric blankets and toasters, tickets to ball games, television sets and stereos, and even a Rolls Royce. Yes, a New York City savings institution offered a Rolls Royce to a depositor who would place a substantial amount of money on deposit for ten years. Banks offer free services to customers, such as tax advice, payroll handling, and so on. These are schemes to override the controls and, as with rent controls, we could think of the market clearing at the "price" that includes the extras.

Another way in which interest-rate controls can frustrate the workings of supply and demand is when they are applied to borrowing rates. When the rate on mortgages, for example, is fixed below the market clearing rate, people are turned down on loans they could afford and would like to have. This happened in the spring of 1980, when many state usury laws prevented mortgage lenders from charging a rate that covered their borrowing costs. A similar experience took place with credit card companies in some parts of the United States.

A further problem with interest-rate ceilings is that when there is rationing because demand exceeds supply at the controlled rates, it is the relatively rich who are given the funds. The young and needy who do not own property to secure the loans do not get them.

What about grain price supports?

Rent controls and interest-rate ceilings keep prices below where they should be. Agricultural price supports work to keep prices higher. Many supports have been removed, but they do serve as an example of a scheme that was aimed at achieving a better outcome than the uncontrolled market but that proved to be a poor system. It is therefore still instructive to examine the effects.

Let us use our maturing imaginations to suppose that the government wants to keep the price of wheat high. How can it be done?

*Can the government keep wheat prices above
their natural levels?*

It certainly can, if it's prepared to buy wheat at a high
price. If some private buyer didn't want to pay the same
high price as the government, he wouldn't get any wheat.
So, if he wanted to stay in business—perhaps baking
bread—he would have to pay the high price also. What this
artifically high price means, in terms of our law of supply
and demand, is that (private) demand would be less than at
the (lower) uncontrolled price, and supply would be larger.
So, at the artifically high price, supply exceeds (private)
demand.

Is the law of supply and demand violated?

No, the law of supply and demand isn't violated because
the government—official—demand plus the private demand, which together is total demand, will still equal the total—all private—supply. Moreover, we can argue that the
price can only stay artifically high if the government *remains*
a buyer. But if you buy year in and year out and don't use up
what you buy, a stockpile will develop. At first, you can de-
fend this practice on the grounds of "national defense." You
can also give some away to poor, needy countries. But unless
you want to keep the price of wheat abnormally low for
about as many years as you keep it abnormally high, the
government will end up with more and more embarrassing
stocks, while the poor will pay very high prices for bread.
Prices are more likely to be held too high than too low, because farmers lobby harder than bread buyers. What is more,
to keep prices low for a consistent time, the government will

have to continue to supply the commodity to the market. The government can do this from stockpiles, but as a non-producer, the government cannot do this for long.

Can unions and restrictive practices violate the law of supply and demand?

Even with unions and restrictive practices, supply will still generally equal demand if we define and interpret the concept properly. But first, let's make it clear that the price we are talking about is the price of labor, which we generally call wages. Our question is: Can unions ensure that wages will be where supply doesn't equal the demand of labor? Unions, if they are effective in negotiating wages with management, can presumably keep wages higher than if there were no unions. (Even *this* is disputed by some, but we'll skirt that issue here.) But if they can maintain abnormally high wages (price of labor), then demand for labor will be less than it would be without unions, and supply will be greater. There will be a glut of people wanting union jobs— as plumbers, longshoremen, truck drivers, and so on.

But why don't the extra people who are so eager for jobs lower their wage demands? It's simply because the unions limit the number of people who are even allowed to get in and be on the scene to do the job, who can enter the factory floor or call at your door. Of course, trade unions are not the only group that controls who can enter the club and do certain work. The doctors' union is called a medical association, and dentists call theirs a dental association. Lawyers have their Bar. The stated purpose is to maintain standards of practice, and they undoubtedly do a good job of that. But, by putting pressure on the market through restricting medical and law school admissions, and hence qualified personnel, they ensure healthy salaries for themselves because there will be fewer people to take care of everybody else's health and legal problems. Again, supply still equals demand, but because the "union" lowers supply, it forces up the price at which the (artificially reduced) supply equals demand.

What are the limits of supply and demand?

In this chapter we have discovered that when we take pains to distinguish between diminishing returns and returns-to-scale, the law of supply will invariably hold. We have also discovered that, other than in very special cases—where consumers get more satisfaction merely from paying more or they judge quality by the prices they pay—the law of demand will also invariably hold. Morever, once we have carefully included all the different aspects of price and governmental or union influences within total supply and demand, the law of supply and demand will still always be valid, except during temporary adjustments to changed circumstances.

But what are these changes and what valuable predictions and understanding can be gained from a working knowledge of supply and demand? We will find that there is virtually no limit to what we can discover.

10

PLAYING WITH
SUPPLY AND DEMAND

*According to the law of supply and demand, when buyers don't fall
for prices, prices must fall for buyers.*

Anonymous

Talk is cheap because the supply always exceeds the demand.

Anonymous

What will make prices change?

With two sides to every price, a supply side and a demand
side, economists divide up the factors that affect prices according to which side they will affect. We will follow this
practice and start with factors changing the supply.

What factors can change supply?

When there is a dominant or a sole supplier of a product,
or else some collusion among the sellers, the supply can be
changed at the seller's wish. For example, when the Organization of Petroleum Exporting Countries (OPEC) decides

that supply should be reduced, then, provided it can ensure that its members will comply, the supply *will be* reduced.

When supply has been reduced, we know the effect. At the original prices there is a shortage of supply. Competition among buyers for the limited available quantity forces up the price. At the higher price, there is an effort to reduce the amount consumed—that is, the volume of demand—and an incentive by other suppliers—those working outside of OPEC—to step up production and search for additional supplies. There is a price at which the reduced, available, overall supply and the demand will be equal, and the lower the supply, the higher that price. This is very visible in the free market for oil that is centered in Rotterdam.

What other factors change supply?

Sometimes the supply will be changed by the weather or other natural or uncontrollable events. This has the same effect on market prices as when they are consciously changed. In Brazil, for example, if widespread frost destroys the coffee crop, coffee prices will rise. There is even a temptation not to wait for unpredictable frosts and, instead, to arrange to destroy some of the crop and profit from the "accident" if the price of coffee will rise sufficiently to offset the fall in quantity sold. There is also an unusual case of an owner of a rare stamp, of which there were only two known copies, who paid a fortune for the second copy and then promptly destroyed it. This raised the value of the remaining copy above the previous combined value of the two stamps. Artists limit the number of lithographs in an edition by destroying the plates for the same reason—that is, to keep down supply and to keep prices up.

Supply can be affected not only by a conscious decision or

a natural event, but also through a change in production conditions. Production conditions will change when there is a change in production costs.

How do costs affect supply?

We have seen that output should be set at a level where marginal costs have risen as high as the market price of the product. Suppose that after this has been done there is an increase in marginal production costs. Perhaps this is because wages or material prices go up—hence raising marginal unit costs above the selling or market price of the product. Losses will be suffered on goods produced at costs higher than the prices at which they can be sold. Two things can be done to remedy this. The firm can either raise the selling price of the product or reduce supply in order to reduce the costs of production. A firm with some degree of monopoly power will raise the price. A firm in a highly competitive market situation will not, on its own, be in a position to do this. Instead, it will reduce supply. This will mean that the price of the product will rise even though the firm cannot by itself pass on a cost increase.

How will costs eventually be passed on to consumers in a competitive market?

The mechanism is relatively straightforward. We start at a price where supply equals demand. The cost of production then goes up. The competitive firm can't raise prices, so it cuts back on production. This means that supply falls below demand. When supply is below demand, the buyers tend to compete for the reduced supply and up goes the price. Producers will happily accept the higher amount. Other producers will do the same thing, and the market price will increase because of the increase in costs.

We note that the price increase offsetting the increase in costs isn't just a question of each producer tacking the extra cost onto the price of what is sold. It is the result of the workings of supply and demand. As we will discover later, it is only a monopoly that can raise prices directly as costs go up. However, the ultimate effect is the same, even when firms are in a competitive situation: cost increases cause prices to go up. This is hardly a surprise. In fact, the economics of supply and demand produces very few surprises—when we have it right.

Are there other examples of costs affecting price via supply?

Examples of cost increases working through to product prices are frequent and obvious. Increases in costs of grain will work their way into prices of margarine and whiskey. Profitability on marginal units of output is cut, supply is reduced, and market prices go up. But sometimes we get more interesting price dynamics. When feed-grain prices increase, it costs more to feed cattle. Farmers slaughter and sell more animals because at the same beef price and higher production costs, losses occur on previously marginal units. The immediate effect of this is more beef on the market, which depresses beef prices. That runs counter to the normal result. We find higher production costs lowering the price of the final product. However, the longer-term effects are as we would expect. The smaller herds eventually result in a smaller supply of beef in the future. And as consumers shop for their favorite cuts of meat and are faced with a reduced supply, they force prices up. The feed-grain price increase will eventually reach your pocketbook.

But how much of the increase will the consumer bear? Will it be all or only a part?

Is an entire cost increase passed along to the consumer?

It surprises many people to hear that only a part of the increase in production costs will reach consumers if final product demand is sensitive to the market price. The argument goes like this: When costs rise, firms produce less. The smaller supply raises the market price. At the higher market price, consumers will make do with less, since this is the nature of price-sensitive demand. Less purchased or demanded means less produced, since, from the forces we have described, supply will equal demand. So a cost increase leaves eventual production below original levels. This happens only because the producers must absorb some of their cost increase. Although they are helped by cutting back output along the law of diminishing returns, they must have higher final unit costs or they wouldn't have reduced production below original levels. Firms absorb some of the extra costs, and consumers therefore face only part of a production-cost increase.

What else will change supply?

We have seen that supply will change because of production costs. Another factor that will change supply is changes in the price of what a firm *could* produce instead of what it *is* producing.

How do prices of alternative products a firm could produce affect the supply?

It is easiest to answer our question with an example. Suppose that a manufacturer of corn margarine needs make only small modifications to turn his factory over to the production of corn-based cooking oil. If corn cooking-oil prices go up because of shortages of safflower or other types of oil, the margarine manufacturer may consider a shift in production if the oil price rises much more than the price of margarine. If many other manufacturers also convert their plants, the increase in the price of cooking oil will lower the supply of margarine. This will mean that the demand for margarine will exceed the supply and the price will rise. We find that an increase in the price of an alternative product will raise the price of whatever else the firm is able to produce: Increases in the price of cooking oil force up the price of margarine.

The supply side is only half of price determination. We must also look at what affects demand.

What factors can change demand?

The important factors that will change demand are income, prices of goods that fill similar needs, prices of goods that are enjoyed only together, and tastes. We shall start with income.

How does income affect demand?

As people's incomes go up, they will demand more. This moves demand above supply, which raises prices. This is absolutely straightforward. The effect of prices of other goods that fill a similar need is rather more subtle.

How do prices of goods filling similar needs affect demand?

Goods that fill similar needs are called *substitutes*. Let us take an example and consider what would happen to the price of lamb if the price of beef goes up.

Since beef and lamb fill similar needs—in this case, to fill our stomachs—as beef prices rise, some consumers will shift to lamb. This increases the demand for lamb, and lamb prices therefore rise. This is not because of a common increase in production costs; it is because beef and lamb are substitutes for one another. In reverse, a fall in prices will lower the demand for and the price of substitutes.

Another example of substitutes is gas for the private car or using public transportation. When the price of gasoline goes up, some people shift to traveling by bus or train. This raises demand for these other forms of transportation, and their prices, if they are free to vary.

At the other extreme are the products that economists classify as *complements*. Complements are products that are used together, such as tennis rackets and tennis balls, bicycles and bicycle tires, cars and gasoline, and ice cream and fudge topping.

How do prices of complementary goods and services effect the level of demand?

When the price of bicycles goes up, according to the ordinary law of demand, the demand for bicycles will go down. When the demand for bicycles declines, so will the demand for bicycle tires. And if the demand for tires goes down, so should their price. We find the price of tires falling when bicycle prices rise. The price of complements move in opposite directions. Similarly, as ice-cream prices rise, people buy less of it and less fudge topping as well. Topping prices decline and those for ice cream go up.

We have seen complement effects at work in the automobile slump of 1980. Over the previous year prices at the gas pumps almost doubled. Since gas and automobiles are complements, the rise in gas prices—as well as general economic conditions of the time, including high interest rates—caused demand for automobiles to decline. This caused the manufacturers to reduce prices by means of rebates that reached as high as $1,000. Again, we find the prices of complements moving in opposite directions.

To summarize, complements are the opposite of substitutes. When beef prices go *up*, both the demand for and the price of lamb will also go *up*. On the other hand, when prices of bicycles and gasoline go *up*, the prices of their complements—bike tires and automobiles—will *decline*. We find that demand for a product can be changed, not just by the price of that product, but by other prices as well. The effect could be in either direction, depending on whether the other good is a substitute or a complement.

This is an impressive list of factors that can change demand. But how about people's tastes?

Do people's tastes affect demand?

Certainly tastes do affect demand. Taste can include virtually anything you care to name. For example, it is taste that explains why people want to shift from butter to margarine or from white to whole-grain bread. It is taste that explains why avocados or artichokes become the vogue and cabbage and potatoes go out of style. When taste raises the demand for a product, for whatever reason, the price will also increase. Tastes will be changing along with everything else.

Does this make life difficult for the economist?

With income, prices of substitutes and complements, tastes, production costs, and who knows what else changing at the same time, an economist frequently does not know what effects will dominate. What he does because of this is to take each change separately. This is called *ceteris paribus*, which means assuming that everything else, or *ceteris* (from etcetera) remains unaltered or *paribus* (from parity). This term is an important part of an economist's vocabulary. You should employ it liberally in arguments to sound like a real economist.

Another Latin phrase that economists like is *a priori*. This is used when an argument is based on theory, before we have empirical evidence. The results in this chapter of effects of incomes, prices of substitutes and complements, tastes, and such are all from a priori arguments. They are educated guesses, based on the theory of supply and demand. When the theory is used well, our a priori conclusions will generally prove to be correct. But they will not be correct if we misuse the theory, as is frequently done with a common error.

What is this common error?

We can show the common error if we take, for example, the following answer that every economics instructor must have heard after asking what happens when demand goes up: "Well, when demand goes up, with the existing amount of supply, pressure among the buyers will raise price. The increase in price causes producers to want to make more because there is more profit at the higher prices."

This is where the answer should stop, because this is the correct conclusion with both higher price and output. Often, however, the answer goes on: "As the producers make more, they must lower their price in order to sell it. The lower price raises demand. As demand rises, the price rises. This encourages more production, so supply goes up, lowering price, which raises demand . . . " and the argument goes on ad nauseam. Sometimes the mistake is more subtle, but the mistake is the same.

Where does this answer go wrong?

Let us try to understand the mistake. It is true that increased demand for a product causes the price to go up. It is also true that, at the higher price, because of the law of supply, producers will manufacture more. But that is where it ends. In this case, *supply went up because prices went up.* It is not accurate to then say that *price falls because supply goes up.* This is reversing what has been said in the previous step, and we can't have it both ways. Never use the causation more than one way around, and you won't go far wrong.

To prove to ourselves that we have the argument correctly, we could take some questions and provide the answers. For example, we could ask:

Why do flights to Europe cost more in the summer?

This question illustrates how seasonal factors influence prices through their effect on demand. We know that it doesn't cost any more for gas, wages, and other expenses to fly a plane a thousand miles in July than it does in November. Yet, charter and other flights to Europe advertised for dates starting in July cost a lot more than those advertised for the winter months. During the summer, more people would like to take holidays in Europe than at any other time of the year. The demand will be higher for holidays in all price ranges.

A price that is low enough to fill the planes in March or April will mean a lot of overbookings by June. When demand is higher, rationing the product—in this case, airplane seats—means the price must rise. That's it. When demand goes up, the price must go up so that we do not have a shortage. At high prices, all available planes will be working, and those who can afford the more expensive summer seats will generally be able to find a carrier prepared to take them. Of course, in the cold of northern winters, the demand for holidays in the warmer climates of Hawaii and the Caribbean will be high, and so will the prices of holiday packages. We find that with a constant supply, seasonal variations in demand cause seasonal variations in prices.

Can supply factors make prices seasonal?

It is supply, in fact, that is the common cause of regular seasonal price variations. During the winter when the available supply of fresh produce is low, if the produce were sold at lower summertime prices, there would be a shortage with supply below demand. The short supply raises the winter prices of the fresh produce that is available. This is so obvious that we need spend no more time on it.

Supply and demand is valuable, and not just for explaining what is intuitively obvious, such as the two examples we have just given, or even those given earlier in this chapter. It is valuable because it helps explain much more puzzling phenomena. It is by no means intuitively obvious why poor harvests will often leave farmers better off or why increases in such overhead costs as rent should not affect prices. It is also not obvious why the value of the labor in a product is not reflected in the product's price, or what economists mean by no "free lunch." With the knowledge we have acquired about supply and demand, we are ready to tackle these more challenging problems.

11

UNRAVELING A FEW ECONOMIC MYSTERIES

Another thing where demand always exceeds supply is sex.
Anonymous

Why are farmers happy when they have a poor harvest?

A poor harvest resulting from generally awful weather conditions would seem to be an unfortunate event for those unlucky farmers whose crops are destroyed or whose output is reduced. It may surprise you to learn that such events as poor harvests can actually make farmers better off. Indeed, when farmers are organized to keep some of their output off the market—even when harvests are good—they can gain by selling less. A certain condition must occur for greater revenues to result from reduced output. This condition involves the value of the *elasticity of demand*.

What is elasticity of demand?

The elasticity of demand tells how much demand will change when the price of a product goes up or down. We have seen in the law of demand that rising prices mean lower demand, but we didn't examine how much lower it would be. Some things will be bought in very similar amounts, even when prices go up or down by a relatively large amount. Salt is an example. The demand for other products will vary considerably on the price. For instance, the sales of a particular brand of flour will likely fall if the price of that brand, compared to other brands happens to go up.

When a 1 percent increase in the price of a certain product causes the quantity purchased to fall by *more than* 1 percent, then we say that the demand for that product is *elastic*. It is considered a flexible, or elastic, demand because increased prices elicit a strong reaction from buyers to make do with a smaller amount. Quantities change by a greater percentage than does price. On the other hand, where a 1 percent increase in price causes the quantity of a product purchased to fall by *less than* 1 percent, it is said to have an *inelastic* demand. We say that demand is inflexible, or inelastic, because when the price is increased, people are so inflexible in their need for the product that they will not significantly reduce the amount that they buy. Economists make an important distinction between elastic and inelastic demand because it is what gives us an explanation for a number of counterintuitive results.

To take an example, during the year 1979, the price of gasoline about doubled—that is, it went up 100 percent. According to the National Petroleum Institute, the consumption of gasoline fell almost 10 percent. This is very inelastic, and we might claim that on the average each 1 percent increase in price is associated with only one-tenth of a percent reduction in demand. On the other hand, the demand for the gasoline of any particular gas station is likely to be very sensitive to the price charged. For example, if a station located near others unilaterally raised prices 2 percent, it might lose 10 percent of its sales—a very elastic demand.

From the concept of elasticity we can understand the condition whereby farmers are better off from poor harvests, or OPEC oil producers are better off by holding back supply. Since the concept is applicable in numerous situations, let's express our question in general terms.

When can lower sales result in higher revenues?

The answer is obvious—when the rise in price associated with lower sales is greater than the reduced quantity that is sold. If the price goes up by more than the quantity goes down, revenues must be higher, because revenues are merely the price multiplied by the quantity sold. This is true only for an inelastic demand, as we have just learned. For example, if Brazil cuts down the quantity of coffee it sells by 10 percent, but gets an extra 50 percent added to the price of the smaller quantity reaching the market (because of frost or economic planning), that country would be much better off. We can now note, though, that this will occur only if there is an inelastic (inflexible) demand for coffee.

Can one farmer increase his revenue by keeping his produce off the market?

The answer to this is a most definite no, and it is because one farmer by himself cannot affect the price of what he sells. He must sell at the same price as other farmers. If he tried to raise his price and supply less, he would sell nothing at all; buyers would buy from the other producers. An individual farmer has what we call a *perfectly elastic demand* for his product. A 1-percent increase in his price in isolation causes a complete reduction in the quantity of his product sold. Remembering that elastic means that the quantity sold falls by more than the price increase, a complete reduction in sales means a completely, or perfectly, elastic demand.

But there must be many situations where market demand is inelastic and where there are obvious advantages in forming a cartel. Why are there so few? The answer is that cartels tend to break up. In addition, they are illegal.

Why do cartels break up, theoretically?

We have seen that higher revenues can be achieved by producing and selling less where there is inelastic demand. Clearly, producing less reduces costs. It follows that collectively producing less can raise revenues and reduce costs. Profits will therefore go up. We should expect to find everyone getting together to profit from a particular kind of cartel. However, as we have said, this is illegal. Antitrust legislation is available to use against those who find themselves tempted to form cartels. But even if cartels weren't illegal, by their very nature they are unstable unions.

Cartels are unstable because each separate, or individual,

producer has good reason to be greedy. At the high prices created by the cartel, he can increase his profit by selling more through undercutting other members' prices. If it is only this individual producer who does this, then the price of the product won't be reduced very much by this behavior. However, every member has the same incentive to increase output. If many individual producers become greedy, they will reduce the market price, thereby reducing the benefits for themselves and all the other cartel members.

Apart from the legal question, the problem with maintaining an effective cartel is that of preventing cheating. It used to be believed that the temptation to cheat is so strong that every cartel will eventually fall to pieces. We have seen that cartels occasionally do survive for many years—witness OPEC. Perhaps, however, they need a noneconomic motive to bind their members.

If cartels—or at least those that survive—are a mystery, then surely another mystery is the fact that fixed costs are irrelevant. A fixed cost is one that must be incurred, and to an economist they mean very little indeed.

Why are fixed costs irrelevant?

Recall from the earlier discussion that firms that take prices as given should produce at a level where marginal unit production costs equal price. The marginal cost is the cost of an *extra unit* of output. If rents or some other item of overhead like interest on debt were to rise, this would certainly raise the average cost of what is produced. But it wouldn't affect the cost of an extra unit that depends on extra materials and extra labor required. Materials and labor are variable—not fixed—costs. Variations in fixed costs leave output unaffected.

Of course, if fixed costs go so high that losses are incurred, the factory will be closed. Then those fixed costs are very relevant indeed. But in terms of the best levels of output, fixed costs don't count. And if this result seems highly mysterious, what about the "free lunch"? To an economist, there is no such thing.

What do economists mean by no "free lunch"?

Economists are not good people to take to lunch. Even if you pay, they'll tell you that, for them, it's not free. They'll say it even when nobody has been kind enough to invite them out. Why do they show so little appreciation for other people's generosity? We will see that it has to do with different levels of opportunity costs.

From the individual's point of view, having lunch requires two expenses. There is the cost of the lunch in dollars, and the time it takes to enjoy it. We all know the age-old cliché, "time is money." Well, it doesn't help save on time even if the other person foots the bill. Even if there's no need to pay, the opportunity cost of having lunch—that is, what we give up to eat it—is the time that we could otherwise have spent doing something else.

Another example is a department store sale, where the best bargains are available to those who wait outside for hours before the store opens. The cheap dollar prices are offset by the opportunity cost of the time spent waiting outside and for some, this leaves them paying a price that is not low at all.

Are there other effects of economizing on time?

While we are talking about the value of time and its part in the cost of goods we enjoy, we can also point out that people with high hourly earnings will tend to minimize the time they spend trying to save dollars. There are even a few economists who will tell you that the high hourly earners will economize on time spent in foreplay. According to the viewpoint of these economists, high hourly earners will substitute for time what is relatively cheap to them—capital goods: a comfortable bed and room, relaxing music, and soft lights.

Isn't this outside of economics?

There is a whole branch of economics that specializes in allocating time, and sometimes they get carried away. There is an excellent parody on the work of these economists in the prestigious *Journal of Political Economy,* normally a serious and highly technical academic journal. In an article entitled "The Economics of Brushing Teeth," an economist, Alan Blinder, writing in the oral tradition of Princeton University and acknowledging the help of his dentist in filling in the gaps in his analysis, draws some not-so-startling conclusions. He manages to prove mathematically that, given certain conditions on the way people gain satisfaction from what they do—in terms of their *utility function*—nobody will spend more than twelve hours a day brushing their teeth. Using data provided by the FBI (Federal Brushing Institute), he explains why waiters spend more time brushing their teeth than chefs. Why? Because the reward from clean teeth to waiters is higher. He also makes the observation that assistant professors brush their teeth more times a day than the more superior ranked full professors: Full professors, who earn more, face a higher opportunity cost and therefore spend less valuable time in scrubbing.

Blinder is having fun with his fellow economists with his tongue-in-cheek writing, but his work is frighteningly close to what some economists are studying. They are getting dangerously close to our bedrooms and bathrooms, and they might already be peeking in.

Are there other aspects to no "free lunch"?

There is another sense in which there is no free lunch. On the aggregate—as opposed to the individual—level, if I get to eat a lot of food, then somebody else can't. If I eat a nice trout or a can of beans, then those things aren't available for some other person. So when we consider the entire world, nothing can be free because the opportunity cost is someone else not having what we consume. You might well tend to agree but wonder about the situation if the food would have otherwise been wasted. You might think that if you hadn't turned up for lunch, the food wouldn't have been eaten, so, on the aggregate level, it was indeed free. Well, in a long-term sense, this is not valid. Let us see it in another living example.

You might hear someone rationalize wearing a fur coat in this way: "The animals whose skins are in this coat were dead before I bought it. No extra animals died for me. Indeed, if I hadn't bought this coat and it wouldn't have been sold otherwise, the animals would have died to no avail. And wouldn't that have been a shame." Surely you can see the flaw in this argument.

Fur coats are made because the manufacturers expect to

sell them. If they don't sell, the manufacturers will eventually produce fewer of them. If you don't eat lunch out, and thus the restaurant ends up with unsold meals, that restaurant will order less food in the future. Eating food that is already prepared and wearing the skins of already dead animals leaves future production and killing unaffected.

There is no sense in which, on the aggregate, things that enter the marketplace can be given away free. Even air—clean air—is not free. We've been learning that lesson for quite a while now. We have to give up cheaper production methods—a real opportunity cost—to keep down air emissions. I'm afraid free lunches cannot exist because people attach value to time, and because goods are scarce.

Do product prices reflect the value of labor?

Many will view it as mysterious that product prices do not usually reflect the value of the labor that's involved in manufacturing a product. If it is not mysterious, it is difficult to explain why so many early economists came to the wrong conclusion. To prove the contention that prices do not have to reflect labor value, we will conceive of some very labor-intensive products. We will create extreme examples.

If some unknown person produced a carefully handwritten copy of an existing novel, would it sell for a high price? What would be the market price of bone shirt buttons that are hand-carved by experienced craftsmen who spend ten hours on each button? Clearly these items will not have great value despite the quantity—or even quality—of labor that is involved. Value, as we have seen, is determined by supply and demand. For high value, we need a good level of demand, as well as a short supply. There might be a short supply of handwritten novels and carved buttons, but they won't be worth much if no one wants to purchase them. Labor theories of value, which used to abound, have gone out of style. They concentrated on supply and forgot demand.

Why are economists generally against using price controls?

If inflation is so evil, why isn't it stopped by the government refusing to allow further increases in wages and prices. Without doubt, wage and price controls can be very popular politically. However, in a free-market economy, they can prove to involve enormous costs in creating economic inefficiency. This is certainly true if they are applied for any length of time.

In our discussion of supply and demand, prices were seen as signals of what to produce and what to buy. If a product is in great demand, compared to supply, the price will rise. This tells the producer of that product that he can make additional profits by providing more. And so the production of what we want will increase. This very clever signaling system has led economists to conclude that freely varying prices make the consumer the king. What he wants, reflected by the price he is prepared to pay, is then produced.

People's tastes change all the time. We want more advanced electrical goods, more extensive forms of travel, and different foods and wines. We are always shifting our demands for what we want to enjoy and therefore, in a free-market economy, the market signals are changing all the time. As we prefer to save time by using air travel, our demands are shown by the amount we are willing to pay for that convenience. This shows the airlines what to provide.

Wage and price controls turn out the lights of the signals that are provided by a free-market price system. They prohibit the movement of relative prices in their effort to control absolute prices. Producers don't know what to produce, and even if they do, there is no incentive to produce what the consumer really wants. Shortages develop in individual areas where increased demand is not followed by an increase in supply. The supply does not change because the price is controlled. We find consumers being rationed by standing in line and paying the price partly in waiting time. Economic inefficiencies begin to abound. We can survive if the control is on for only a limited time, but beyond that, the inefficiencies involve a massive cost.

Is there ever a time for wage and price controls?

Some sort of case can be made for a temporary adoption of wage and price controls if the government has been fighting to reduce inflation in some other way. When undertaking other cutbacks to beat inflation by trimming government programs and growth in the money supply, expectations of inflation might be brought in line by adopting controls for a limited time. If inflationary expectations are reduced by the wage and price controls, wage demands will moderate. Other policies used to fight inflation can then work without causing high unemployment. But wage-price controls cannot be tried many times to reduce inflationary expectations, without also taking the other steps to reduce actual inflation.

*Does supply and demand apply equally to
necessities and luxuries?*

If incomes go up by 10 percent, people are unlikely to buy
10 percent more of everything. In particular, when ample
good food and a decent home have been provided, some extra income will go into more food or in paying for a larger
home, but most people will not spend a full 10 percent more
on these essential or necessary items. In other words, demands for basic necessities such as food and housing are
likely to rise less than the percentage by which income goes
up. Similarly, when incomes decline, people do not reduce
their demand for necessities by as much as their incomes decline. A 10-percent change in income means a less than 10-
percent change in demand for necessities.

But just as people spend less of their income increases on
some items, they will likely spend more on other things. For
instance, with 10 percent more income, they might spend 20
percent more on travel, theater, and other luxuries of life.
Economists distinguish necessities from luxuries by the size
of the corresponding *income effects.* When spending on a
product rises by a smaller fraction than income, the effect is
small and the product is called a necessity. When the reverse
is true and spending on a product rises by more than income, the income effect is large, and the product is considered a luxury.

Can income effects be negative?

Generally, as people earn higher real incomes, we would
think that they would buy more of everything. So even
though income effects would be small on some goods, in-

come and demand in general would at least move in the same directions. Well, there are some goods for which income effects are negative. For these goods, higher income makes people buy less. These goods are called *inferior goods*.

An inferior good is an item such as bread or potatoes. When people earn higher incomes, they can afford to consume more meat and cheese, and since they get their nourishment from these more exciting foods, they need less of the staples. As a result, higher incomes lead to a fall in demand for the inferior goods. This effect can, in certain circumstances, be so powerful that it produces something known as *Giffen goods*.

What is a Giffen good?

Sir Robert Giffen observed that when potato prices went down, very poor people actually bought less of them. This runs counter to the law of demand, by which people should demand more goods as their prices fall. The Giffen good, however, does not violate the law of demand. Rather, it is a case where a powerful income effect dominates the conventional behavior based on the law of demand.

When the price declines on an individual product, we really have two things happening at once. The relative price declines, but there is also an increase in real incomes. When the fall in price is on an item that is a very major part of our normal budget, it gives us an increase in real income. The fall in relative price makes us want to purchase more, and the accompanying income effect will usually reinforce this. However, when the income effect is negative, it offsets the relative price effect. Although a lower price usually means a higher demand, when the product is an inferior good there is a lower demand because of higher real income. When this income effect dominates, we have a Giffen good—lower price causing lower demand. It's a fascinating possibility, but it is not likely to be of any importance outside of eighteenth-century Ireland.

Do income effects ever go by another name?

Ernst Engel, who is not related to Friedrich Engels, Karl Marx's benefactor and long-time friend, made a name for himself by plotting income effects. A graphical relationship between income and the amount spent on different products for the market as a whole became known as an "Engel curve."

With a number of mysteries unraveled and an understanding of supply and demand, we can move on to an account of different types of market settings. Markets differ according to their competitiveness, and this gives rise to important differences in prices paid by consumers.

12

MONOPOLY, OLIGOPOLY, COMPETITION, AND PRICES

With uncontrolled competition, man gets to exploit man. Under monopoly, it's just the opposite.

Anonymous

There's no resting place for an enterprise in a competitive economy.
Alfred P. Sloan

What markets are distinguished by economists?

Like all scientists, the economist tends to love taxonomy, which simply means classifying and putting things in groups and under headings. Botanists do it with plants, zoologists do it with animals, psychologists do it with people, and economists do it with markets.

The most important type of market for the economist, because it's so easy to study, is the *perfectly competitive market*. A perfectly competitive market is one where there are many sellers of precisely the same good, where all buyers know every seller's price, and where any new seller who wants to get involved faces no barriers to entry.

The first important feature of a perfectly competitive market is that all sellers must charge precisely the same price. Since the buyers are assumed to know all the sellers' prices, they would all buy from the cheapest seller if the prices were to differ. Any seller charging more than the minimum price would not be able to sell anything, and so they are all forced by competition to charge the same, which is the minimum price.

The second important feature of a perfectly competitive market is that no seller can make an unusually high profit. If the activity were to be extremely profitable, the assumption of no barriers to entry would mean that there would be many who were eager and able to join the industry. Their eagerness to get involved and get customers would keep prices down. Since more new firms would want to enter as long as profits were unusually high, they would continue to bring down prices until the profits were "normal" for the amount of effort and risk involved. Therefore the perfectly competitive market is characterized by all prices being the same and also low enough so that only "normal" profits remain.

The other market settings the economist distinguishes are monopoly, duopoly, oligopoly, and the hybrid, monopolistic competition.

Are monopoly, duopoly, and oligopoly different types of business board games?

What, precisely, distinguishes these different market settings? A *monopoly* is one firm that controls an industry. In general, monopolies do not occur naturally. The chief requirement is a barrier to the entry of new firms. There probably are situations where one firm would be all that survived even if there were no imposed barriers, but as often as not, monopolies can't occur unless the government offers some sort of "charter," which keeps out other firms that would like to get involved. The post office, and local electric utilities are examples of monopolies; if you don't like the service, there's not too much you can do about it.

Some people say that the examples of monopolies we have given are examples where competition would be ineffective. Without getting into that debate, we can note that since entry is restricted, profits could get high without the force of competition from eager new firms bringing them down. That is why it is extremely important for the government to regulate state-granted monopolies or else to allow competition that avoids the need for government regulation.

A *duopoly* exists where an industry consists of two firms. The existence of two firms does not mean that there is little competition. They could be in fierce competition with each other. An *oligopoly* is the natural extension of a duopoly, where an industry contains several firms, but not a very large number. Automobiles, aircraft, steel, and many other industries fit into this category. Competition can exist here and it can be keen, but antitrust laws are needed to make sure that the few firms don't get together and start rigging prices and acting like a monopoly. There have been a few much-publicized cartels, and they have done no one but themselves any good.

There are other market settings that are less well known. One that is very common is monopolistic competition.

What is monopolistic competition?

Monopolistic competition is the market setting that exists when there are many firms, full buyer information, and no barriers to general entry (which are all features of perfect competition), but with products that are somewhat differentiated. Branded products like detergents would fit into this category. There's nothing stopping a new firm from entering the detergent business, and there are already quite a few participants. A glance along the supermarket shelf gives the buyer a quick idea of the various prices. Yet, because of brand preferences and loyalties, each producer has a little flexibility in the price he can charge. This market category would be very broad within manufactured goods.

A *monopsony* is a monopoly on the *buyer's side*—that is, it is the situation where there is only one buyer of a product. Economists are generally a lot less worried about problems on the buying side because there are usually many buyers and therefore plenty of buyer-side competition. Can you think of a product with a single buyer? It's not easy.

Which type of market setting gives the lowest price?

Economists have never been fond of monopolies—unless they happen to be employed by one, in which case *their* monopoly is O.K. When there is only one firm involved in the market, it is in a powerful position to hold back production to keep up the price. If the price can be forced up by more than the percentage of reduction in quantity sold, revenues and profits can be increased. We have called this situation— prices rising more than the reduction in sales—an inelastic demand. Since no profit-maximizing monopolist would fail to raise prices if higher profits would result, we know that no monopolist would set output or price at the point where the demand is inelastic. Prices will always be raised when demand is inelastic—with consequent higher profits—until the demand is no longer inelastic. If it is not inelastic it is elastic. Therefore monopolists must always be at a point of elastic rather than inelastic demand.

Competitive firms are not in a position to withhold supply; if they do, someone else will fill the vacuum. They therefore produce a greater output collectively than would a monopoly in the same situation. But a bigger collective output must mean charging a lower collective price or all the output would not be sold. This, then, tells us that monopolists always charge more than competitive firms would in the same market and they produce less.

Do some firms have more than one price for a similar product, and if so, why?

If it costs $10 to produce each of ten items a firm manufactures, there might be two people who want the item enough to pay $20 each, another two who are prepared to pay $18, another two $16, another two $14, and the last two $12. If the firm can charge only one price in order to sell the ten items it produces, that common price will have to be $12. If the firm charges more than that, some people won't buy and revenues will be reduced. Selling ten items at $12 brings in only $120. The firm would be much better off if it could charge each person the maximum he or she is prepared to pay (Two people would pay $20, two would pay $18, and so on down to the two people who would pay $12 each). If it could do this, the firm would end up with a total of $160. But if a single price must be charged, the best price is $12 each. It is better to sell ten items at $12 rather than only eight at $14. However, this is far less valuable to the firm than charging each buyer what he or she will pay.

A firm that can charge different buyers different prices, according to what they are prepared to pay, is called a *discriminating monopolist*. Such a firm discriminates among the buyers, not on the basis of race and sex, but according to the desire for the product, which is reflected in the maximum price they are willing to pay.

Are there discriminating monopolists in the real world?

There are no discriminating monopolists who can charge everybody the most they are willing to pay. The reason is that it is difficult to figure out what people would pay and to prevent those prepared to pay a lot from nevertheless trying to get away with paying less. When a person pays less than he or she is prepared to pay, economists call the gap *consumer surplus*. You might want a pair of pants so much that you would pay $50 when you can actually get them for only $40. You will have a ten-dollar consumer surplus.

Even though monopolists or oligopolists can't use price discrimination perfectly because they can't keep people with big needs from trying to pay less, they can discriminate to some extent. Many department stores will sell an item at a high price upstairs and at a low price in the basement. They hope that those prepared to pay more—often the rich—will not want to be seen in the basement. Rather than risk losing the bargain hunters because of the high prices upstairs, the stores try to capture them in the plainer surroundings of the basement.

Airlines use price discrimination whenever they can. Richer people who are often prepared to pay more to travel do not like to take the chance of not getting their chosen flight, so airlines charge a higher price for reserved seats. The poorer population, including students, would travel much less if they had to pay full fare. The airlines therefore "discriminate" in their favor by charging them a lower fare but at the cost of their having to stand-by and risk missing the flight they want. The airlines count on the fact that the more affluent passengers will not try for the stand-by seats; they would rather pay more and be sure of getting the flight they want. Charter rates offered to vacation travelers are another way of discriminating in favor of those who might not fly at full fare but who are willing to accept the restrictions of advance bookings and limited choice in travel times. By determining and discriminating among different types of travelers, imposing restrictions, and charging appropriate prices, the airlines can raise their revenues, increase their load factors, and boost their profits. Price discrimination does exist, even though the situations and extent are limited by the ability to identify and separate different market types.

Are there any natural monopolies?

There are economists who argue that a monopoly can sometimes be better for the public than perfect competition. It is said that even though competition can lower prices, sometimes it can result in wasteful duplication and eventually higher costs and prices, as in the case of the postal service.

Imagine a world with a whole collection of postal delivery and collection companies. If the morning mail consists of four or five items, and if they happen to be sent through four or five different postal companies, you might have that same number of mailmen walking up to your door. That would seem to be wasteful. Or imagine competing telephone companies within a single area. In order to receive calls from people subscribing to different companies, you might have to hook up to all of their lines. The sky and ground would be filled with lines going everywhere. The same goes for the power lines from utility companies. If different people on the same street bought electricity or gas from different suppliers, each street would be filled with power cables and gas lines from various companies, unless they operated by sharing.

How can you cope with natural monopolies?

Natural monopolies are hard to avoid and so we have to learn to live with them. There are ways, however, to make that coexistence reasonably easy to bear.

Monopolies always have an incentive to raise prices if it will increase profits, even if it happens to be at the public's expense. What must be done, then, to make sure that the prices they charge do not bring them abnormally high profits? Public-utility regulatory commissions have generally been charged with the task of requiring utilities to rationalize their prices and to watch that their profits do not become excessively large.

There is an alternative way of regulating that helps avoid the red tape and bureaucracy that regulatory bodies can entail. Natural monopolies can be periodically sold to the highest bidding firm. If, for example, there is to be just one privately run, duty-free shop at an international airport, the airport authority can put up for bid the exclusive rights for ten years of operation. The highest bidder, who is prepared to meet the service requirements, can be granted the license or right. The money paid by the bidder can be returned to the public who use the service in, we hope, some equitable way. The firm that gains the monopoly should not earn an abnormally high return on its investment. If there were obvious abnormally high returns stemming from the monopoly rights, other firms would bid up the winning bidder's price until the return on the capital invested, including the payment for the right, was reduced to a normal amount.

What circumstances are required for a natural monopoly?

The post office, public utilities, and such tend to have in common what we have called earlier *increasing returns-to-scale*. This, we recall, is the situation where production on a larger scale, with more of all the factors of production, means operating at lower unit-production costs. When we have increasing returns-to-scale, overall production costs are reduced by having a large producer operating at low unit cost, rather than a number of smaller producers at higher cost. It is said that the laws of survival will ensure that monopolies develop naturally when there are increasing returns, because the firm that gets largest the quickest will have lower costs and prices, thus forcing the others out of business.

Where do we find increasing returns? There probably are increasing returns in the public utilities, including postal services, but there are also increasing returns in many private industries. Because of the advantages of large computers, it is argued that banking shows increasing returns. Because of advantages in long production runs, the automobile industry could also show increasing returns.

What limits the size of firms when there are increasing returns-to-scale?

Banks in the United States cannot experience unlimited growth because they are generally restricted to operating full service branches only within their state or their county, even if they would like to venture outside. In some locations they are limited to only one branch. Large automobile companies cannot grow and squeeze out their rivals without fear of antitrust action. It pays for them to ensure that weaker members survive, even if some have trouble because they do not know what behavior is necessary for survival. Chrysler Corporation proves the value of learning economics in order to survive.

There is an additional force that limits size even when the production conditions show increasing returns-to-scale. This is the constraint of managerial ability. As firms grow, they become more and more difficult to manage. Inefficiencies crop up and go uncorrected because nobody sees them. When growth goes beyond managerial ability, costs begin to rise, even if production conditions continue to show increasing returns. Because of limits on the ability to manage larger units, many industries consist of a number of firms.

Do monopolies and competitive firms respond to the same market signals in the same way?

When the public develops a greater desire for an item and is prepared to pay more, the profitability of that item goes up. All firms producing that item, whatever the market setting, will respond by supplying more. Similarly, if the costs of one of the inputs into the production of an item were to go up, all firms would economize on that item. For instance, if wood prices were to rise vis-à-vis bricks, house builders would use less wood and more bricks. It doesn't matter what type of market setting exists when determining the direction of response to these stimuli.

Is inventiveness encouraged by competition?

It has been shown by economists like MIT's Robert Solow and by Edward Denison of the Brookings Institution that approximately half of the growth in the American standard of living—when it was growing—could be attributed to technological advance. Because of the importance of technological change, it is relevant to ask whether it is likely to be stimulated more by competition than by monopoly. A theoretical case can be made either way. It is instructive to examine both sides.

Free competition requires that firms constantly keep up to date in what they produce and in the production methods they use, or they will be unable to survive. However, what is the value of discovering a better production methodology—an innovation—or a new product—an invention—if there are many other firms who will immediately "borrow" your idea and employ it against you? Therefore, gains from an invention or innovation will be short lived in a competitive environment. To avoid this disincentive to inventiveness, we must grant inventors and innovators exclusive patent rights to use their ideas. In addition, some argue that since monopolies have larger profit margins, they can more easily engage in research and development—R & D—as well as more easily profit from it.

The question of whether more inventions and innovations

occur with monopoly than with competition is a sticky one which does not yield a straightforward answer. There is merit to both sides and there is even another side that argues that inventions respond to chance and do not have an economic basis. Indeed, much governmental and university research is not directly economically motivated. Others say that necessity is the mother of invention. Suffice it to say that even monopoly and oligopoly might have some virtue to recommend them if they lead to more R & D yielding inventions and innovations, and hence economic growth.

We can provide a more definite answer regarding competition versus monopoly in the degree to which they produce the maximum output to enjoy. The self-interest of free and uncontrolled competition produces a remarkable result: Its output makes people better off than any other output. This is the leading argument for encouraging competition. Self-interest provides optimal economic behavior, most of the time anyway.

13

THE POWER OF
SELF-INTEREST

Economics does not apply to the female of the species: a woman without principle always draws interest.

Anonymous

It is a socialist idea that making profits is a vice; I consider that the real vice is making losses.

Winston Churchill

What drives the competitive economy?

While the government tries to influence the shape of the competitive economy, it is private decisions and actions that are the determining factors in most of what is produced and the way it is divided among consumers. The many separate firms and individuals making their supply and demand decisions do so in a way that provides consumers with what they want. When the demand for a product goes up, this pushes up the price and encourages firms to produce more of it. And so the consumer finds more being supplied when he or she demands more. It is self-interest on the part of firms and consumers in a competitive economy that causes this to happen.

Self-interest takes the form of efforts by firms to maximize profits and by consumers to maximize satisfaction. Together these efforts to maximize, which have selfish motivation, guide the many unconnected elements of the economy as if they were being directed by an invisible hand.

The invisible hand belongs to Scottish economist Adam Smith, and an understanding of it is well within our grasp. In his celebrated volume, *An Inquiry into the Nature and Cause of the Wealth of Nations* (1776), Smith described the miraculous workings of the price system. He was fascinated by the way that scarce goods (such as fine silks) in a free-enterprise economy command such a price that people wish to purchase only the limited amount that is available, while, at the same time, more plentiful goods (such as potatoes) also get sold without much being left over.

The consumer who wanted to buy spices and teas that had come all the way from the Indies and the Orient could find them in Scotland and England because somebody was prepared to go to a lot of trouble to provide them. Traders would buy carefully selected spices and teas in those far-off lands, charter ships with crews, and have them sailed to the British Isles. They would then distribute them to fine stores in such areas as London and Edinburgh, where people wanted to enjoy good tea and spices. It was as if some invisible hand had stretched halfway around the world and dropped these exotic goodies right where people wanted them. Of course, the invisible strength in that invisible hand is what today is perhaps too visible and is called *profit*. The motivation for profit guides the uncontrolled and unconnected elements in the world's free-market economies toward producing and distributing what the people of the world want to buy. The other system, occurring in a less-free part of the world, might be characterized as being guided by an iron fist.

What is involved in maximizing profits?

Surprisingly perhaps, profit maximization doesn't involve fleecing the public and trying to raise your price continuously. That can be a quicker way out of business than keeping your prices down. High prices, if they are not followed by other firms selling a similar product, could mean a dramatic loss of demand and a quick exit from the game. Neither does maximizing profits mean paying subsistence wages to all who do the work, because if other firms also want to take their share, they'll be trying to hire your workers away. If you don't pay the going rate, you'll soon be left with nothing to sell.

Maximizing profits is achieved by producing the output at which the extra or *marginal revenue* from selling an extra unit is just equal to the cost of that unit, which we have called the *marginal cost*. When we have a competitive market—which we recall means having many firms—the marginal revenue is the price at which the product is sold. If we sell an extra necktie at $10, we will increase our revenue by $10 if we do not have to lower the price to sell it. The profit-maximizing rule, therefore, is to produce to the point where the price equals the marginal cost, a rule that we derived earlier. It is well worth repeating how we reached this conclusion, because it is a direct extension of this rule that shows why competition is superior to monopoly.

Why does profit maximization involve equating price with marginal costs, in competitive markets?

When the price at which an extra product is sold exceeds its cost—the marginal cost—the profits must rise from that extra unit of output. If it costs $8 to produce an extra silk necktie, and it can be sold for a price of $10, it would be silly not to produce and sell it. A profit of $2 can be made on the extra tie because profit is the excess of revenue over cost. We know that if profits are to be maximized, the firm will never want to stop producing at a level where the price (in our example, $10) exceeds the marginal cost (in our example, $8). By producing more, profits will be larger.

But, on the other hand, if the firm were to keep adding to production until the price falls short of marginal cost, profits would decline. For instance, if production were raised to the point where it cost $12 to produce an extra necktie (perhaps because workers must be paid overtime rates), but the tie can be sold for only $10 (which is the price at which the competitive firm can sell whatever it produces), profits would fall. By producing a necktie at a marginal cost of $12 and selling it at a price of $10, the firm will lose $2 on this necktie. The firm might still be making large profits overall, but why reduce profits by producing so much that the last unit costs more than it contributes to revenues? This would not be profit-maximizing behavior.

Now we have the key. We have seen from our $10 versus $8 case that we don't want to stop at a production level at which the sales price *exceeds* marginal cost or we will not be maximizing profit. We have also seen from our $10 versus $12 case as mentioned previously, that we don't want to stop at a production level at which the selling price is *less than* marginal cost. Again, this would not be maximizing profit. How much would we then want to produce in order to maximize profit? The answer is that production should be set at the point where the price for the extra unit *equals* marginal cost. This follows since we should produce more when price exceeds cost and less when price is less than cost. The only other point left is where they are equal.

Of course, we would want some profit, even on the last unit sold, so its marginal cost should be a little less than the marginal revenue from its sale. But any profit is fine, however small. Accepting only a tiny profit on the last item produced doesn't mean that total profits won't be very large. Earlier items that cost less to produce could contribute to a very handsome total profit. Since we should add to production as long as even the tiniest profit is made from extra units—or else we are not making the *maximum* profit—we can claim that profit maximization requires an output where price and marginal cost are equal.

To demonstrate the advantages of competitive markets, we need to combine the profit maximization of competitive firms with the maximization that is done by consumers. Consumers want to maximize their satisfaction.

How do consumers maximize satisfaction?

To satisfy our many and diverse desires, we must determine where we should direct our scarce and therefore valuable resources. For most of us as individual consumers, this means allocating our incomes to try and achieve the maximum level of satisfaction from our constrained or limited means. We must choose what we buy carefully so as not to waste by buying too much of those items we need less of. How should we decide on the appropriate amounts of each item that we should buy? We can describe the behavior that will maximize consumer satisfaction by returning to our necktie example.

If we do not have any up-to-date neckties, we might, for example, get $20 worth of satisfaction or *utility* from the first new tie we buy (with $10 of this being consumer surplus if the price is only $10). A second new tie might give $15 worth of extra satisfaction or utility, a third $10 worth, a fourth $5 worth, a fifth $2 worth, and so on. Now, if ties have a price of $10 each, and we have this particular scale of satisfaction, we will want to buy at least one new tie. Surely, at a selling price of $10 each and with $20 worth of extra satisfaction or utility, we will be extremely happy with the first tie we purchase—and enjoy $10 consumer surplus. A second tie, with $15 worth of extra satisfaction, will also be bought and give $5 consumer surplus. We might also want yet one more, because with $10 worth of satisfaction at a price of $10 it is still worthwhile. We will not, however, buy four ties. Given the alternative ways of spending money, with only $5 worth of satisfaction from a fourth tie and a $10 price we have negative consumer surplus; we would be smarter to buy something else, perhaps some new socks or an economics book. We conclude, then, that people buy until the price they pay, vis-à-vis the alternatives that exist, is just equal to the extra satisfaction or utility that the product gives them. The "vis-à-vis alternatives" is necessary because, to be precise, consumers equate relative amounts of satisfaction with relative prices. But to avoid complicating it, we can say that consumers equate the extra satisfaction with the price. This is as true for ties as it is for everything else.

Can we tie together maximization of profit and satisfaction?

Indeed we can, and without getting into knots. In doing so, we come up with what we claimed earlier, that uncontrolled competition is better than monopoly.

We know that competitive firms equate the selling price with the marginal cost of production. In our example, these are both $10 at a given output. We have also now seen that we, as consumers, buy until the extra satisfaction that is derived from our purchases is equal to the price that we pay, both again $10 in our example. We have two things that are both equal to the price. The consumer buys until the extra satisfaction equals the price, and the firm produces until the point where the marginal production cost equals the price. But if the extra satisfaction and the marginal costs are *both* equal to the price, then they themselves must be equal. The extra satisfaction and the marginal cost are equal, both $10. This happens if consumers are maximizing satisfaction in a world where firms are competitive and are maximizing profits. What uncontrolled competition will achieve is that the cost of providing an item—its marginal cost—is equal to the satisfaction that it provides.

Can we do better than produce to the point where marginal cost equals consumers' satisfaction?

Suppose that the economic system that is in effect directs us to continue producing more of an item, past the point where the cost of making it equals the satisfaction of the person who buys it. As we produce more and more, the cost of getting extra production out of our existing number of machines and factories will begin to rise. To continue with our necktie example, the cost of an extra tie might rise to $12. This follows from our law of diminishing returns. And, on top of rising costs, as we produce more and more, the satisfaction derived from an extra unit would begin to decline. The first glass of cold juice on a hot day is wonderfully satisfying. The second might be too. But a third? A fourth? A fifth? The satisfaction of extra units of almost anything will eventually decline. The satisfaction from extra neckties, as more are produced, will fall below $10, perhaps to $5. So with production costs rising and satisfaction on the decline, if we produce beyond where production costs are equal to satisfaction, the resources going into the production will cost more ($12) than the value of the pleasure that is given to someone ($5). What a waste this would be! The resources should have been used elsewhere.

Suppose the reverse were to occur. Suppose an alternative economic system causes production to be at a level where the cost of resources for making that item are less than the satisfaction it yields. That is also wasteful. Why? Because we shouldn't stop at a point where the costs are less than the satisfaction someone obtains. More resources should be devoted to making this item because they are less costly than the pleasure and benefit the item gives.

There you have it. If you produce *more than* the amount where marginal production costs equal satisfaction, it's wasteful. If you produce *less*, it is also wasteful, in that opportunities are being missed, our now familiar *opportunity cost*. It must follow that the best economic system is one that produces to the point where marginal production costs equal satisfaction. And that, we now know, is what uncontrolled competition will achieve.

Why doesn't monopoly maximize happiness?

A monopoly can select the price it wants to charge, and to sell more it must lower prices. This is unlike a small competitive firm that sells whatever it produces at going market prices. But if a monopoly must lower its price to sell more, the extra, or marginal, revenue is less than the unit price of what is sold. This is because to sell an extra unit the price on the other units must also be reduced. Let us take an example.

If ten ties are sold when the price is $10.00 each and the price must be reduced to $9.75 to sell an extra tie, the extra, or marginal, revenue from the extra unit that is sold is not $9.75. This is because the monopolist is also selling each of the previous ten ties for 25¢ less. The extra revenue from selling an extra tie, with 25¢ less on ten previous ties is $9.75 less $2.50, or $7.25. This marginal revenue of $7.25 is less than the market price of $9.75.

A monopolist maximizes profits by equating marginal revenue and marginal cost. If he gets a marginal revenue of $7.25 from lowering his price by 25¢ to sell an extra tie, it is worthwhile to do this as long as it costs less than $7.25 to make the tie. He will not lower price by 25¢ to sell an extra tie if the marginal cost of producing it is more than $7.25. He therefore stops at the point where marginal cost and marginal revenue are equal. But remember, to a monopolist, the marginal revenue is below the product's price because he must lower prices to sell more. And since the marginal revenue is equated to the marginal cost, if the marginal revenue is below the price, the marginal cost will also be below the price.

In maximizing their satisfaction, we will recall that consumers equate the price with the satisfaction they derive. If the product is made by a monopolist, we have just learned that the marginal cost will be below the price. It follows, then, that when goods are produced by monopolists, marginal cost is less than the price, which, in turn, is equal to the consumers' satisfaction. The marginal cost is therefore less than the satisfaction derived. That is an inefficient situation. Why should production stop at a level where the cost of providing the goods is below the satisfaction that is derived? No, we should produce more. Monopolies, we discover, produce insufficient amounts of goods from the point of view of society. Competitive production levels cannot be improved upon by a controlled or planned system or by a monopoly. This is an important conclusion.

Well, does free enterprise work so wonderfully in actual practice? As sound and solid as our case has been, there are potential flaws in the practice of this system that can result in excesses and shortfalls of production or consumption. It can sometimes provide too much, when there's environmental deterioration associated with the production or consumption of products, and too little, when there are environmental improvements. We can see this if we ask the following question.

When does uncontrolled competition fail to produce a balance between costs and satisfaction?

When we describe the "best" economic system as the one where costs are all being equaled by the benefits or satisfaction derived, we of course mean *all* of the costs and *all* of the benefits. But what if not all of the costs are being paid by the people involved in the production? Or what if some of the benefits are derived, not by the person making a purchase or outlay, but by others who get a "free ride." When we examine the world as it exists, we see that such situations do occur.

Consider the cost of driving an automobile. Among the

chief variable costs—those varying with the number of miles driven—is the cost of gasoline. Let us assume that we drive our cars until the cost we personally pay for the last mile we choose to drive is equal to the benefit or satisfaction we personally derive. Let us call the cost we personally pay the *private cost* of driving a mile. We might as well then call the benefit we personally derive the *private benefit* of the mile.

The private cost is not the entire cost. There is also a *social cost*, besides your private cost. The social cost includes having to live with extra air emissions and the extra congestion that you cause. The extra congestion is a cost every driver pays when it takes just a little longer to reach a particular destination because *you* are on the road.

If you drive your car to the point where the private cost equals the private benefit, we know that at that point the social costs will exceed the private *and social* benefits obtained. By not considering the wider social costs, you will drive "too much" because the costs including those of air pollution and congestion borne by society exceed the total benefits.

We can take a second example of overdoing it—an example more in the vein of maximizing profit rather than maximizing satisfaction—if we consider the production of steel. The private cost of producing steel does not include the cost of dirtier air near the producing facility. But if steel producers continue manufacturing until they reach an output where their private marginal cost equals the price of their product, they will produce too much. The social cost of the steel, which includes the dirty air, will exceed the price and social benefit derived. Free competitive enterprise is socially inefficient when there are gaps between the private and social costs of activities.

Are there cases where we produce too little?

Indeed there are, although such cases are probably less common than activities that are excessive. The conscientious person who provides a beautiful front yard for all those who pass by to enjoy will himself obtain only part of the benefit that we collectively derive. If this person equalizes the private cost and private benefit from a well-maintained garden, the social benefit will exceed the social cost. From the viewpoint of society, more of such items should be provided. Only if a person could in some way be rewarded for the pleasure he or she gives the rest of us would the level of activity be correct.

How do economists refer to the problem of differing private and social values?

When people drive their cars, the extra social costs of pollution and congestion borne by society as a whole are *external* to the driver who imposes the costs, except to the extent that he is a tiny part of the whole society. The costs that are external are appropriately called *externalities* or *spillovers*.

When externalities provide benefits to all of us, as in the case of a beautiful rose garden, we say there are external *benefits* or *positive* spillovers or externalities.

*Can we eliminate the excesses and deficiencies
caused by externalities?*

To get rid of the excessive level of driving or production
when there are external costs imposed on society, we must
eliminate the externalities. We must make the individual
consider the social cost of his activity by making him pay the
price. In this way we can *internalize* the externality. If the
amount of pollution and congestion from driving an automobile depended only on the amount of gas used by the individual, internalization could be achieved with a gasoline
tax. If pollution from steel production depended only on the
level of output, we could apply a tax on production.

Can we internalize social benefits?

When a conscientious gardener tends the flowers and
shrubs in front of his home—or, for that matter, when the
appropriate authorities do the same in public places—we
have the case of a *public good*. Public goods are things from
which we can all potentially benefit and for which we need
pay no more to enjoy more of. We can look at our neighbor's
flowers as much as we wish and stroll in the beautifully kept
up park whenever we like, and we will pay no more. Thus,
public goods are difficult to "price." Only if home owners
could charge the public looking at their gardens would we
get more well-tended gardens.

In the case of parks, we have a public good for which we
could charge per unit of use (per visit), but which we have
instead frequently chosen to finance out of general tax revenues. When this is so, people who get great benefit are being subsidized by those who rarely or never visit the park.

What other public goods are there?

One major public good is national defense. We are all assumed to benefit from it, and we provide its financing through our taxes. A high-income individual generally pays more than one with a low income, yet the former might get less satisfaction from being defended. We could argue that this is unfair. It would be fairer if we all paid according to how much benefit we derive. But imagine the problem here. Suppose everybody were asked, "How much benefit do you get per year from being defended?" and we were then charged according to our answer. Everyone would tend to answer, "Nothing," even if as individuals we derived very high benefits. Why? Because the benefit would be the same whatever we as individuals were forced to pay. Therefore, why pay anything at all? Clearly we can't proceed in this manner and we must use some other means, however imperfect. General taxes based largely on income provide one alternative in which we pay according to means, not according to benefits.

We have discovered that perfect competition will maximize national welfare only if there are no externalities. But in addition, the firms and consumers must behave rationally with the firms maximizing profits and consumers maximizing satisfaction.

Do firms really maximize profits?

Firms don't know their marginal costs and revenues. Nevertheless, economists go around assuming that they do. If they didn't believe this, they wouldn't be able to make their living promoting such lovely and clear theories as those we have just described. We do have to admit, however, that those firms that behave most closely to the theories we have given will do the best. They are the ones that most easily survive and enjoy the largest profits. In that sense, the theories do give us useful predictions.

Richard Cyert and James Marsh are behavioral economists. They believe that business executives in real-life situations maximize such things as sales, people employed, their own job security, managerial salaries, or the size of their offices. Profit maximization for their shareholders—even over the longer term—is a very narrow goal for a giant enterprise in which ownership and control are separate. Economists have continued to write as if these other goals don't exist. If we wish to be open-minded, we have to admit that profit maximization takes place alongside other goals. In cases of conflicting goals, management decides on the path to take.

How much rationality is there?

Economists cannot proceed without rationality. It is the essence of what we have been describing. Efforts to maximize profit and consumer satisfaction are based on rational behavior, as well as on self-interest. The beautiful workings of free enterprise as a method of providing the best alternative requires rationality. But clearly, many people do not always make rational decisions, at least not when they are viewed retrospectively. Ultimately, whether free-market allocations should be encouraged or some alternative system should be used depends on the rationality of individual firms and consumers versus the rationality of the government if it were to intervene. But what do we know of the rationality and effectiveness of government control?

Does economic planning work well?

We in the West have by no means cornered the market in good economic minds. However, language and ideological barriers tend to be very high, so we do not know many intimate details of the planning procedures used in Soviet economics. We do know something of Soviet economics from the work of Leonid Kantorovich, which has reached sufficient people outside of the Soviet Union to win a Nobel Prize for Kantorovich. We also know a little from another Nobel winner and former Soviet, Wassily Leontief. Leontief has done research in a variant of planning economics and has a certain following.

Soviet economics plays down the crucial role of prices that is the centerpiece of even the mixed economies of Europe and North America. Central economic planning requires a careful study of what is available and what things are to be selected as national priorities. The feasibility of achieving the competing priorities with what is available is then carefully analyzed by computing inputs and outputs. Certain adjustments can then be made. The mathematics of this process can be quite complex, but the major difference from the price system of the West is in the centrally determined needs.

A free-enterprise, market-oriented economy allows consumers to express their needs through the signal of prices. When a central planner tells us what we can have, many might find their preferences far different from those allowed. We know from our earlier demonstration—showing that competition achieves the best level of output to meet individuals' needs—that central planning cannot do better, unless there are external costs and benefits. Since there *are* externalities, we mix free enterprise and government control. We therefore have *mixed economies*.

Is there an economic theory of mixed economies?

Economics teachers still base their lectures on supply and demand. The aesthetic appeal of the straightforward but nevertheless powerful rules never fails to impress students who are eager to learn. But what is the role of supply and demand in our mixed economy? There are so many instances where the law of supply and demand is not allowed to work and determine price. We have already spoken of governmental price supports, union power, and minimum-wage laws. And there are even more cases of regulated price. By concentrating on the role of supply and demand, we can learn a lot, but we miss some of the wider procedures for determining price.

I happen to believe that the free-price system is being replaced by the fair-price system. How much should you pay someone like a nurse? The free-price systems says at the point where supply equals demand. It says that if you don't pay enough, there's a shortage of those willing to do the job. This shortage will force hospitals to pay more, which will stimulate the supply. Even ignoring the problem of training and recognition lags, this is no longer the way prices are set.

Wages of nurses and others are not set by supply and demand. When negotiations occur, the question has become "What is fair?" What is fair is determined by what other people get. If secretaries earn this and teachers earn that, then a nurse should receive such and such. It doesn't seem to matter that, at such a price, there is a shortage or a glut of willing employees. What's fair is fair, and this has a limited amount to do with freely determined price.

There are many examples of the fair-price system replacing the free-price system: It's unfair for anyone to work below a minimum wage. It's unfair for anyone to pay more than a certain rent. No farmer should get less than a fair price for his product. An oil company should not make an unfair profit. Doctors shouldn't make unfair incomes.

Personally, I don't like the fair-price system, but we must all accept that it exists. Even though we can answer some of the questions with supply and demand, we must rewrite a lot of economics to discover, for example, "What is the mechanism that determines what is fair?" Or "What role do fair prices play in the inflationary process when fairness means more wages each year, quite independent of productivity?" It's not clear if these questions have any answers at all, but it isn't fair to write an economics book like this without pointing them out.

IV

International Economics and Exchange Rates

14

DIFFERENT WAYS
TO DO TRADE

Economists do it on demand.

Written on a T-shirt

I heard a very warm debate between two professors, about the most commodious and effectual ways and means of raising money without grieving the subject. The first affirmed the justest method would be to lay a certain tax upon vices and folly, and the sum fixed upon every man to be rated after the fairest manner by a jury of his neighbours. The second was of an opinion directly contrary, to tax those qualities of body and mind for which men chiefly value themselves, the rate to be more or less according to the degree of excelling, the decision whereof should be left entirely to their own breast. The highest tax was upon men who are the greatest favourites of the other sex, and the assessments according to the number and natures of the favours they have received; for which they are allowed to be their own vouchers. Wit, valour, and politeness were likewise proposed to be largely taxed, and collected in the same manner, by every person giving his own word for the quantum of what he possessed. But as to honour, justice, wisdom, and learning, they should not be taxed at all; because they are qualifications of so singular a kind, that no man will either allow them in his neighbour, or value them in himself.

Jonathan Swift

Is international finance very difficult?

Probably the most frightening and foreign element of economics for the noneconomist is the world of international high finance. An understanding of the notions and issues of this world that is inhabited by such a few fabulously powerful "gnomes" and central bankers need not be the sole domain of those who play the massive-number games. The notions and issues batted around the international financial community can be understood by anyone who can spend money or find his or her own way to the bank. So, let's ask some of the questions that might have been on your mind for a long time. Let us start out by asking about exchange rates.

How are exchange rates determined?

There are two major systems in the world through which exchange rates have been determined. These are the *fixed exchange-rate system* and the *flexible exchange-rate system*. We'll take them in turn, and we'll see how they go about generating the *exchange rate* between currencies, which is just the amount of one currency—say dollars—it takes to buy another currency—say pounds sterling (£). We will see that there is no need to feel intimidated if the dinner or cocktail-party conversation turns to the plight of the dollar or the strength of the yen on the world money markets.

How do fixed exchange rates work?

Fixed—or to use the more correct tern, *pegged*— exchange rates are set by the central banks. For the sake of argument, if the pound sterling were to be fixed at $2 for £1, that exchange rate would be set by the Bank of England. Now, of course, the exchange rate of $2 to £1 isn't going to remain at that rate just because the Bank of England says so. To prevent the price of the pound from falling below $2 when there are a lot of people who want to sell pounds, the Bank of England must buy up all the pounds that others don't want, and it will have to pay $2 for each of them. Thus, no one will ever accept less than $2 for his pounds because he or she knows that the Bank of England will always pay that much.

To be sure that the Bank of England can always *buy* pounds at $2 each, it must have a good reserve (foreign-exchange reserve) of dollars on hand. It must ensure that no one ever has to worry about the bank's resolve or ability to buy its pounds at the fixed exchange rate of $2 each.

To prevent the price of pounds from going above $2 when lots of people wish to buy pounds, the Bank of England must be willing to *sell* all the pounds sterling that people want at the fixed price of $2. If it does that, no one will ever pay more than $2 for £1 sterling. Why should they if they can always buy them from the Bank of England at a price of $2? Of course, since the Bank of England can print its own money, there should always be plenty of pounds in its vaults if people are set on buying them.

There you have it. Fixed exchange rates are determined by the central bank standing ready and willing to buy and sell its own currency for another currency (here the British pound sterling and the U.S. dollar) at the fixed price it has chosen. In that way, the exchange rate can remain at the price the central bank fixes, until it wants or is forced to fix a new price. The fact that "fixed" does not mean that the exchange rate will never change is why calling this system a "pegged" system is a little more appropriate. We will stick with the more commonly used "fixed" terminology, however.

Do fixed exchange rates have to be set in terms of U.S. dollars?

The answer is no. We can get an exchange rate of $2 to £1 sterling if both the dollar and the pound sterling are pegged to some third currency or commodity instead of to each other. There was a time when a commodity was used for currency-value determination, and that commodity was gold. The system that fixed exchange rates in this way has been called the *gold standard*.

How does a gold standard fix the exchange rates?

Instead of the Bank of England declaring that £1 is worth $2, let us suppose for the sake of argument, that the bank says £1 is worth one one-hundredth of an ounce of gold. The price of gold, then, is being fixed by the Bank of England at £100 sterling per ounce of gold.

Now, at the same time that the Bank of England sets the price of gold at £100 sterling an ounce, let us suppose that the U.S. government sets the price of gold at $200 an ounce. Just as with currency, the United States must be prepared to buy any gold that is offered to it at $200 an ounce and sell any amount demanded at that price. If it stands ready to buy and sell whatever is offered or demanded at a price of $200 per ounce, no one will ever sell for less because they can always sell to the U.S. government. Similarly, no one will ever pay more than two hundred dollars for an ounce of gold when they can buy it at that price from the U.S. government.

What do these fixed gold prices mean for exchange rates?

If the Bank of England stands ready to purchase and sell gold at £100 per ounce and the U.S. government stands ready to buy and sell at $200 per ounce, the exchange rate between dollars and pounds sterlings must be $2 to £1 sterling. We can best see why this must be so by showing what would happen if the exchange rate were *not* $2 to £1.

Suppose that the commercial banks in the international financial markets were asking $2.50 per £1 sterling. Could this be the exchange rate between dollars and pounds sterling? If it were, a sensible individual—say an American—could do the following, which we call *arbitrage*. He could take $200 and buy an ounce of gold from the U.S. government. He could then send that ounce of gold across the Atlantic and sell it to the Bank of England for £100. He could then bring home the £100 and sell them to the commercial bank for its exchange rate of $2.50 per pound. The American arbitrager would thus get $250 for his £100. The investor, who began with $200, realizes a handsome fifty-dollar profit merely by making a couple of transactions. If the investor had been richer and had started with $2 million, he would have made a profit of $500,000. Of course, the arbitrager would have had to pay for shipping the gold to England, for wiring the money home, and for exchanging the pounds sterling for dollars, but these would represent a relatively small expense, especially as a fraction of the larger deals.

It should be clear from the arbitrage we have just described that the international financial market will not offer more than $2 for £1 sterling when gold is £100 an ounce in England and $200 an ounce in the United States. If the market did offer more than $2 per £1, the foreign-exchange dealers would soon run out of dollars and would end up with piles of pounds as everyone went through the arbitrage process, acquiring pounds in England and then selling them for dollars in the United States.

Now, it should not be difficult to see that the commercial banks will also never set the exchange rate at less than $2 per £1. If they did, they would be faced with the process we have just described, only working in reverse. They would be swamped with dollars and would run out of pounds. The only exchange rate the bankers in the international money market could maintain would be $2 per £1. So, if the British and the Americans set their currencies to the price of gold, they would, at the same time, be setting the exchange rate between their currencies.

Does the "international money" have to be gold?

No, the item that the central banks use in fixing their exchange rates can be anything. It could be some type of money created by a world-scale international financial organization, for example, *special drawing rights* (SDRs).

What are SDRs?

SDRs are an "international money" that, rather than being manufactured or printed by any single central bank, have been "printed" by all the central banks through their association in the International Monetary Fund (IMF). They are backed by all the assets of the IMF, which used to include lots of gold, but still includes plenty of hard currencies. They are created by merely crediting every country's account at the IMF in return for the country's own money. You and I, however, will not be given a chance to own any.

SDRs are just ledger entries. Any reserve medium will work as long as we have faith that it will work, even if it is based on stars.

What is a star standard?

A number of years back, a magazine, which I've never heard anyone admit to reading and which you'll find on the racks at the checkout line in your supermarket, announced that Fort Knox—and the New York Fed—didn't have as much gold as they said they did. Perhaps it had been stolen. Well, that isn't the sort of story that you'd like to spread abroad, even if the magazine made a living on stories far more sensational than this. Some members of the U.S. Congress, who obviously peek at these magazines while standing in line at supermarkets, demanded a complete investigation. They were taken deep into the vaults for proof that indeed there were many shiny bars neatly stored away underground.

But does it really matter if the gold is there? Isn't what matters what people believe? Under the gold standard, central banks settled imbalances between themselves by moving gold, which each held at the New York Fed, between their different storage areas. They never actually checked their vaults to count their gold reserves. They took the word of the Fed that the gold was there.

But what would have happened if the gold had never even existed? The financial system will work just fine as long as we believe that the gold exists. Financial systems, like banks, are based upon trust. If trust is present, you need no precious metal or anything else. But this gives us an interesting possibility.

Suppose we were to allocate ownership of a large number of the stars that we could never reach, at least not with existing technology. Suppose each country were told that it owned so many celestial bodies and that an account was being kept. These assets, if you like, were created from thin air, rather like SDRs are. Countries could settle their debts by moving around ownership of the stars, rather like moving around gold. This could happen at the ISF—the International Star Fund. We could allocate extra stars every year to facilitate extra needs. Each currency would be worth so many stars, which would determine their exchange rates: £1 million sterling per star and $2 million per star means $2 per £1. What a lovely financial system. As long as countries accept stars as payment it would work. And, remember, there is a fixed supply, just like gold.

Gold has been used as money far longer than stars, so it is more likely to work as a reserve base. Flexible, or *floating, exchange rates*, on the other hand, do not require reserves.

How do flexible exchange rates work?

Flexible exchange-rate determination, unlike the complicated fixed-rate processes we described with price setting by the central banks, is simplicity itself. Flexible exchange rates are determined by the demand for and supply of each currency in the free market. Central banks are supposed to do nothing. The price of each currency is determined in the same way that the prices of oranges, carrots, and woolen sweaters are determined. Prices are set so that the supply and demand for each currency are equal. The process is exactly the same as the supply-and-demand process for anything else in which the government has little involvement, although you might have to tax yourself (excuse the pun) to think of very many examples!

What exchange sytem exists today?

Most major currencies, such as the British pound, the Canadian dollar, the deutsche mark, and the Swiss franc, are flexible and float against the U.S. dollar. Some currencies within the European Economic Community (EEC) are fixed to each other within a narrow range—the *snake*—but the situation is often changing.

If exchange rates are truly flexible and are determined in the private market for foreign exchange, then there should be no changes in central bank holdings of foreign-exchange reserves. This is because the central banks wouldn't be involved in the foreign-exchange market.

Is the dollar fixed or flexible?

It doesn't make much sense to ask if the U.S. dollar is on a fixed or flexible exchange-rate system. If the foreign currencies, such as pounds and marks, are flexible or floating vis-à-vis the U.S. dollar, then clearly the dollar must be floating vis-à-vis these foreign currencies. If the number of dollars per pound is allowed to go up and down, so must the number of pounds per dollar since they are the reverse of each other, or reciprocal. The only thing the dollar had been fixed to has been the price of gold. This is no longer so.

The world was on a gold standard until the Depression. In

1944, after a conference in Bretton Woods, New Hampshire, the United States agreed to fix the value of the dollar to gold—at $35 an ounce throughout the 1950s and 1960s— while other countries fixed the values of their currencies to the U.S. dollar. The International Monetary Fund and the International Bank for Reconstruction and Development both grew out of this conference. The Bretton Woods System broke down in the 1970s and gold prices were freed. By 1978 gold played no role in a largely flexible exchange-rate system.

Does the government ever stay out of the foreign-exchange market?

Despite the protestations of numerous governments on numerous occasions that they are going to allow the exchange rate to be determined in the free market, the temptation to get involved is often too great. The problem is that the people who stand ready to buy and sell currencies under fixed exchange rates are highly paid bank employees. They don't have very much to do when rates are flexible and are determined in the free market. When they get bored, they start to get involved. The problem is that it's hard to fire high-ranking central bankers when you're a high-ranking central banker yourself.

Are flexible and fluctuating exchange rates the same thing?

Let's get something absolutely clear. Flexible exchange rates mean that the rates are *free to change*. They do not *have to fluctuate*. For that reason, people who refer to the system of free-market (flexible) exchange-rate determination as a "fluctuating" system are not only using the wrong terminology, they are also being misleading. There is no such thing as a fluctuating exchange-rate system. There are fixed exchange rates and flexible exchange rates. People who use the term fluctuating rates are usually enemies of flexible rates and are sneaking in a bit of free advertising for their view. Try pulling up a know-it-all who insists on referring to "fluctuating" rates. You'll knock him over in one blow if you repeat what I've just said, and you'll be absolutely right. You might also knock some people over if you said that persistent balance-of-payments surpluses are a bad thing. But before we show how this must be true, we should explain the nature of the balance of payments and trade.

What is the balance of payments?

Simply stated, the *balance of international payments* is the difference between receipts of residents of a country from foreigners, and payments by residents to foreigners. We cannot, however, leave the definition at that. There are numerous different yet potentially relevant *excesses* of this kind and, at different times, we could have an interest in them all. The two major categories are, however, the *balance of payments on current account* and the *balance of payments on capital account.* We might say, even if it's corny, that it's a capital idea to give each a separate account.

What is the balance of payments on current account?

This is the balance that most readily comes to mind. It is primarily made up of the excess of exports over imports of goods and services. A surplus means that a nation's residents are receiving more for their exports than they are paying for imports from abroad. A deficit means the reverse, that imports exceed exports.

The goods component, when taken on its own, gives the excess known as the *merchandise balance* or the *balance of trade.* When we add services, we move toward the balance on current account. Residents receive and make payments for vacations abroad; for the sale of financial, transportation, and consulting services; and for many other "invisible" items of this kind. Since these give rise to foreign-exchange supplies and demands in the same way as payments and receipts for "visible" items such as grains, automobiles, and oil, they must be added to the goods entering trade to obtain the balance of goods and services combined. Another major "invisible" service payment is the service of debt that occurs in the form of interest and dividends that flow both to and from other countries. If we finally add items of funds that get transferred, such as private and government gifts, we have the surplus or deficit on goods, services, and transfers combined. This is the balance of payments on current account. To this must be added the balance of payments on capital account for the overall balance.

What is the balance of payments on capital account?

A good part of the international demands and supplies of a nation's currency come not as part of payments on items of current trade, but rather as payments for financial and real claims. If a foreigner buys an American firm, stock, or bond, payment must be made and this requires the purchase of U.S. dollars on the foreign-exchange market. But this is a demand for dollars that is no different than the demand for dollars to buy American grain, machines, or other currently produced goods and services. Similarly, if an American buys a foreign firm, stock, or bond, the required amount of foreign exchange must be bought, which means that American dollars be sold. The difference between payments made abroad, and those received from abroad, on account of these capital or investment items, is the balance of payments on capital account.

What is the balance of payments?

If anything remains clear, it should be that there are many balances of payment that serve different ends. We must be extremely careful that we select and interpret the right one. The overall balance of payments—*the* balance of payments— is the sum of the balances on current and on capital account. But people are often imprecise and will be talking about one or the other of these two components or else about the balance of trade or merchandise. Get used to paying attention to precisely what people say and ask whether it is the total, the trade balance, the current account, or the capital account. You will find that a remarkably large number of people do not understand these differences. Yet, a balance-of-payments surplus in one of these accounts could easily coexist with a deficit in another account or an overall deficit. Being careful can make all the difference in the world.

Why may surpluses be bad?

Now that we have described the various types of balances of payment that exist, we can explain the statement we made before we began. Let us think of a surplus in the balance of trade, which means the exporting of more goods abroad than we buy abroad to bring home. A trade surplus means more American grains, cars, and other physical products for foreigners to enjoy than foreign-made things for us to enjoy at home. But you wouldn't want to do that for too long. Why provide more American products for others to enjoy than the amount of foreign goods we enjoy in return? It is an absolutely excellent idea to exchange our items for those that others produce particularly well, but you wouldn't want to provide an excess to those abroad on a continuing basis. Balance-of-trade surpluses are a bad thing if they continue for too long.

In case you are wondering how a trade surplus could continue to occur, remember that the balance of trade is only a part of the current account, and to this we must add the capital items before the whole balance of payments is obtained. It is possible to have surpluses on trade offset by deficits elsewhere in the accounts, and if the trade excess is offset by an accumulation of foreign exchange, think what this involves. We provide grains and cars and other machines and, in return, we get pictures of foreign heroes on colored paper, which get locked away. Alternatively, we don't get the foreign currency and instead get an increase in deposits in a foreign bank account, which is a ledger entry without pictures. Foreign money and bank accounts are good things to earn through balance-of-trade surpluses only if they are later used to buy and enjoy goods produced abroad, but this requires a *deficit* in trade at some future date.

Are deficits a good thing?

If surpluses aren't good, then how about deficits? Well, trade deficits are not good things either, because they mean a country is living beyond its means. A deficit in the balance of trade means that the country is enjoying the consumption of more goods than it is producing, and it is obtaining these extra goods by importing more than it is exporting. This, just as for an individual, must be financed by credit, and inevitably the time will come when credit is no longer available. Trade deficits can mean more than trivial amounts of consumption of goods we do not ourselves produce.

To take an example, consider what a $22 billion per annum trade deficit means for the United States. This is an amount that has been exceeded a number of times and is therefore very realistic. A 22 billion-dollar trade deficit, when divided by the 220 million-person population of the United States, means $100 per American individual, or $400 per family of four. Therefore, in a year with a trade deficit of $22 billion, each American family, on the average, enjoys $400 worth of goods that Americans not only didn't produce but didn't cover out of export revenues. Deficits allow us to live well beyond our means.

Should we aim for balance?

Since surpluses aren't good, because we would be supplying others with what we produce, and since deficits aren't good, because we would be living beyond our means, we should hope to achieve a balance in the balance of payments. That isn't to say that we should become upset with deficits and surpluses in particular years. It just means that the deficits and surpluses shouldn't be allowed to become large and should on average cancel out. But how can this be achieved? Can it be achieved by having the correct exchange rate?

What exchange rate will achieve a balanced balance of payments?

There is a particular foreign-exchange value of a currency at which the balance of payments or the balance of trade will indeed be balanced. Values higher than this *equilibrium* exchange rate will mean balance-of-trade or payments deficits, and lower values mean surpluses.

If, for example, the U.S. dollar is priced very high vis-à-vis other currencies, then U.S. exports will be expensive; the dollars will cost a large amount of foreign currency, meaning high prices for American goods for sale abroad. Similarly, when the dollar is priced high this means that American dollars will obtain a relatively large amount of cheap foreign currencies, cheap at least in terms of dollars. Cheap foreign currencies mean cheap imports. It follows from these effects that a high-priced dollar means few exports and many imports, which will contribute toward a deficit in the balance of payments. Alternatively, a very low-priced dollar in terms of foreign exchange means many exports and few imports, thereby providing a surplus. Clearly, if a high-priced currency means a deficit, and a low-priced currency means a surplus, then somewhere in between there must be a balance, or equilibrium, exchange rate.

Will the equilibrium rate hold?

Many economists find it difficult to believe that the government will be able to find the exact rate of exchange at which there will be a balance of international payments. Since the rate at which there will be balance will be changing all the time, a fixed, or pegged, exchange rate is likely to be wrong most of the time. Flexible rates, which change continuously so that supply and demand for various currencies are equal, will always give us balance. That's why many economists who trust the market more than the government tend to support flexible rates. Flexible rates mean a "balanced" balance of payments.

What do rate changes mean?

Changes in exchange rates, as well as affecting the balance of payments, will affect the standards of living in different countries, in both absolute and relative terms. This can be seen in two different ways.

When, for example, the dollar falls vis-à-vis foreign currencies, imports coming into America cost more. We must therefore spend more for desired goods, which lowers the American standard of living. This is an absolute decline. There is another perspective—viewing standards of living in relative terms. Suppose that an average American worker earns $20,000 per year, and that an average German worker earns DM40,000 per year. If the exchange rate is 50¢ for each DM1, the German's income in dollars is the same as the American's, with both at $20,000. If the dollar falls in value against the mark, it takes more dollars to purchase a mark. Suppose the dollar falls in value so that DM1 costs 60¢. This means that DM40,000 is worth $24,000. The American income will be lower than the German income in terms of dollars, whereas before they had been equal. If we were to rank standards of living by putting average incomes into a common unit such as the dollar, then when the dollar falls in value, so will the relative position of the United States. Of course, putting everything in dollar terms doesn't take account of costs of living in different countries, but our example does show that declining currency values mean an absolute and relative decline in living standards.

What do we call changes in exchange rates?

When we are on fixed, or pegged, exchange rates and, for example, the Bank of England decides on a lower value of its currency against the dollar, we say that the British pound is *devalued*. Alternatively, if the Bank of England raises the value of the pound, it would be *revalued*.

When exchange rates are flexible we tend to use different terms. A fall in the value of the pound means that the pound *depreciates*; it is a passive event compared to the more active devaluation, which requires a move by a government. An increase in foreign-exchange value with flexible rates is an *appreciation*. Many people, including a number of economists, do not distinguish devaluations from depreciations or revaluations from appreciations. Just remember that devaluations and depreciations mean a fall in value, and revaluations and appreciations an increase, and you will be fine.

What is gained from international trade?

International trade allows different countries to specialize in what they do best. Bananas should be grown where it's hot, computers produced where workers are smart, cameras and stereos where workers are conscientious, wheat where there's good soil, and economics should be learned everywhere. In deciding which countries should produce what, an *absolute advantage* by being able to do something more cheaply is not necessary. All that is required is *comparative advantage.* This is the discovery of David Ricardo, and it can best be explained by asking a question that will also show the difference between absolute and comparative advantage. "If the world consisted of just Europe and the United States, and the United States were better than Europe at producing industrial goods and much much better at producing grain, will the Europeans be able to produce and profitably sell anything in America?" David Ricardo proved not only that Europe would be able to produce competitive industrial goods, but that in exchanging them for American grain, Europeans and Americans would both be better off.

It would not be counterintuitive to conclude that if Europe is better at producing industrial goods and America is better at producing grain, then both would be better off if Europe concentrated on industrial goods and America on grains. That's easy enough to believe. But what happens when America has an absolute advantage in both? How can there be a gain in having Europe do anything? Well, there you have it. It must be better for the world as a whole for Europeans to do something rather than nothing. And if they are to do something, it might as well be the thing at which, in relative terms, they are less bad at doing—that is, they have a *relative*, or *comparative*, advantage, even if it is an absolute disadvantage. But if the world as a whole is better off with Europe doing something rather than nothing, then there must be some way of distributing things so that both Europe and America, which in our example *is* "the world as a whole," are better off.

Now be honest. Did you really get the correct answer? If you did, it's a shame you didn't get it before Ricardo or you would be a famous economist. You would not be as famous as Ricardo unless you had also made numerous discoveries about the theory of rent and currency. Ah, well!

Even if we aren't likely to all be great economic theorists, we might like to understand some of the more practical aspects of the foreign-exchange markets. For example, we might wish to learn about speculation and dealing in currency futures and forward exchange.

15

MAKING MONEY IN FOREIGN EXCHANGE

It would be too ridiculous to go about seriously to prove, that wealth does not consist in money, or in gold and silver; but in what money purchases, and is valuable only for purchasing.

Adam Smith

If theories, like girls, could win beauty contests, comparative advantage would certainly rate high.

Paul Samuelson

Is it easy to become rich through international financial dealings?

Understanding how the international financial system works is one thing. Knowing how to make it work for *you* is another. Well, there's no quick and easy way to learn how to get rich on the foreign-exchange markets, even though many fortunes have been won—and lost. However, there are things that the average businessman—and even the not-so-average man in the street—can do to save money and worry. The most easily used technique for saving money and worry involves the *forward-exchange contract*, so we will start out by explaining this.

What is a forward-exchange contract?

A forward-exchange contract is an agreement between two parties to exchange one country's currency for another currency at a specified date in the future, and at a rate that is agreed upon when the contract is drawn up. *Forward exchange* refers to the fact that the actual exchange of one currency for the other is not to take place until some time in the future, perhaps three months or even a full year later. For that reason some of the contracts are called *currency futures*, although these generally refer to agreements covering a limited number of dates in each year, come in large lump sums, and are traded only on special markets. In general, though, all that changes hands when the parties agree on a forward-exchange deal is a forward contract.

Usually, a forward contract will be on a standard form. In essence, it might read: "We, the First Bank of Fat City, agree to sell the person named below DM1 million at the exchange value of DM2 per $1 with delivery and payment to be made six months from the date of this contract."

Now, if six months from the date of the contract the exchange rate is 60¢ for DM1, the holder of the contract should be wearing a smile, and a new suit. When he delivers one-half million dollars to the First Bank of Fat City, he will be given DM1 million. If a DM1 is worth 60¢, he can turn right around to Fat City Bank, or any other bank, and sell his DM1 million for $600,000—making $100,000 profit.

At the time that the forward-exchange contract is drawn up, the exchange rate might go either way. Suppose the exchange rate existing six months after the forward agreement was made happened to be only 40¢ per DM1. Now the person holding the contract would find it very hard to wear a smile, and might not even be wearing his shirt. When he pays out his one-half million dollars for DM1 million, all his DM1 million will fetch him if he trys to sell them is

$400,000—incurring $100,000 in losses. To help ensure that payment is made under these circumstances a *margin* is required.

What is the margin?

When the contract in the preceding example is written up, the party issuing the contract will likely demand that the other party leave on deposit with it, for example, $100,000. The issuer of the contract knows it can take what may be lost by the other party (and won by them) out of this amount. The $100,000 (20 percent of the value of the forward contract of $500,000) is the margin. Usually margins are a smaller fraction of the contract size—5 or 10 percent—but they vary according to who you are, whether you pressed your suit, and the color of your collar.

Now can I speculate?

If you happened to think that a particular foreign currency—we can think of the deutsche mark again—was about to rise in value, you could buy deutsche mark bank notes, but would this be a good strategy? First, buying bank notes involves paying extremely large *spreads*. The spread is caused not by overeating, but by the commission fees the bank extracts, and this could easily be equal to several percent of the value of the purchase. Your deutsche marks would have to appreciate several percent for you to just break even. Second, while you are holding the bank notes you are forgoing interest earnings that you might otherwise have received.

Okay, then, holding bank notes is not too smart. What, then, is a better strategy?

If you think the deutsche mark is going to rise a lot in value, you could agree to a forward purchase of deutsche marks with a bank. If you deal with a sizable amount of money (say, more than $50,000), the spread will be quite tiny. What is more, all you have to lay out at the beginning is the margin, and you can even earn interest on this, because the bank will put your margin in a secure type of investment. Unfortunately, though, if your bank also happens to believe that the deutsche mark is going to rise a lot in value, you will get no bargain. The price you will have to pay for delivery of deutsche marks in the future will be higher than the price existing at the time you enter the contract, and the price will have to increase for you to just break even.

Are forward-exchange contracts risky?

Forward-exchange contracts should be left to those with iron stomachs. The risks you face are fantastic. If you are required to post a 10 percent margin, a mere 10-percent unfavorable move in the exchange rate would have you losing your entire margin. There have been many times when 10 percent moves have taken place within hours, or even less. Imagine putting $50,000 up and seeing it gone after you blinked your eyes. Of course, things can go in your favor if you're lucky, but remember that the bankers are very smart, and they price the forward contracts in such a way that it takes more than luck to beat them. If you feel sure that a certain currency is going to increase in value, you can also be sure you will have to pay a higher price for forward or future delivery than you would for immediate delivery. If you don't have to pay a higher price for forward delivery, there are probably some pretty good reasons for being cautious.

Having established that you should be as cautious when speculating in forward-exchange contracts as you are when playing with fire, we should ask when forward contracts can actually bring peace of mind. Well, there are two groups that can use forward contracts to ease their worries. One group consists of those who import and export, and the other group is made up of those who borrow and invest abroad. Let us start with the importers and exporters.

How can importers and exporters use forward-exchange contracts?

Unlike you and I when we go shopping, businessmen never have to pay for a purchase immediately. If an order is placed for a piece of high-technology German electrical equipment and invoiced at DM100,000, payment is not likely to be required for quite a number of months. It is not at all uncommon for manufacturing and shipment to take several months and then for trade credit to be granted for a month or two after delivery. The problem then, is that if you know that in about six months you must pay the German manufacturer DM100,000, how do you know how many U.S. dollars you will be paying? If the deutsche mark rises in value, the number of dollars you must pay for the equipment will also rise. For example, if the deutsche mark goes from 50¢ to 60¢, the cost of your machine goes up from $50,000 to $60,000— quite a jump. But this is where forward-exchange contracts come in very handy. By buying DM100,000 prior to the payment date at the same time that the order for the equipment is placed, you can take away all the foreign-exchange risk. If you buy the deutsche marks at 50¢ each, you'll have to pay $50,000 regardless of what happens to the value of the deutsche mark. Indeed, since you know that you can establish a predetermined dollar price in this way, the existence of forward contracts allows you to compare prices of domestic producers and different foreign producers when no exchange risk is present. It must be remembered that by buying the foreign exchange beforehand, you not only avoid the chance of having to pay more, but also the chance of having to pay less, as would happen if the deutsche mark fell in value. In that sense forward-exchange contracts and currency futures allow you to avoid being a speculator when you want to be just an importer.

In the same way that an importer might want to buy foreign currency forward, an exporter might wish to sell foreign currency forward. For example, an American producer selling equipment to Germany and expecting to receive DM100,000 after six months might wish to sell them before hand to avoid the risk of speculating on how many dollars they would bring.

Do the banks take risks?

The banks that issue forward contracts can themselves avoid speculating by offsetting those selling a foreign currency with others buying it. In this way, any agreement to buy foreign currency from one party is matched by an agreement to sell the proceeds to another party.

*How can borrowers and investors employ
forward-exchange contracts?*

The second group that we mentioned who might find forward-exchange contracts useful is made up of those who
borrow and invest abroad. For instance, an American investing in German bills or bonds that are valued in deutsche
marks stands to lose in terms of U.S. dollars if the deutsche
mark falls in value. If, however, the bills have a maturity
that is not too long and the investor sells forward the
deutsche marks that are due at maturity, he will receive a
known amount of U.S. dollars at that time. Similarly, someone borrowing abroad who has to repay the loan in foreign
currency the next year can buy the needed amount of currency on the forward-exchange market. The exchange rate
existing on the forward contract will then apply when the
debt must be repaid, regardless of what the exchange rate is
at repayment time.

Forward-exchange and currency contracts rarely go
beyond two years ahead. Any avoidance of risk—which is
called *hedging,* or *covering*—that requires going ahead more
than two years can be achieved by borrowing and lending.
If, for example, a payment must be made in Germany after
five years, a five-year bond that matures on the correct date
could be purchased. But this is not the place to delve into
these details. What we have said about forward contracts and
how they can be used to hedge, or cover, as well as to speculate, should go a good way toward showing that the world of
international high finance is not as frightening—or as foreign—as it might at first seem. You might even find it
fascinating.

Can speculators destabilize the exchange markets?

One of the major arguments used against the adoption or continuation of flexible exchange rates concerns the suggestion that speculators can destabilize the foreign exchange market. This means that speculators can cause wide swings in the value of a nation's currency according to their feelings at any moment in time.

To see whether speculators can destabilize currencies, we must answer this question: Can the speculator make the movements in currency values—the exchange rates—wider than they would otherwise have been? Only if the variations in exchange rates are raised by speculative activity can we say that a speculator can destabilize currency values.

Knowing what we do about supply and demand, how can the speculator make a currency value fall by more than it would have otherwise? He must sell when the price is low. How can he make the price go higher than it might otherwise go? He must be buying when the price is high. But let us stop here. Sell low and buy high? This is the recipe for a quick exit from any speculative game. To be destabilizing in the way we have described, the speculator will lose money.

If, on the other hand, the speculator is to come out ahead, he must buy low and sell high. Buying at low prices helps keep up the floor price, with prices above where they would otherwise have gone. Selling high keeps down the ceiling price that there otherwise would have been. This money-making scheme therefore keeps exchange rates moving through narrower swings than would otherwise occur, even if the money moves so quickly that it gets *hot*.

What is hot money?

Hot money is money that has no home. It burns holes in pockets of "gnomes" and moves from country to country as fast as it can travel along the international cable or radio waves. But, as we have seen, these speculative funds help keep exchange rates in a narrower range when they are moved to profit those whose money knows no home. But what about that sparkling home for tired money—gold?

Is gold the universal money?

It has been called a "barbarous relic" by Lord Keynes and the "common whore" of mankind by William Shakespeare, but there is little doubt that gold is the most universally acceptable form of exchange and that most people would enjoy having it hidden in the closet. It is a particularly attractive metal that is a superb electrical conductor, is malleable, and doesn't corrode; but this isn't why it is so generally acceptable and desired. It is desired because others also desire it. That probably seems circular, and indeed it is. What makes a good money is acceptability, and thousands of years of using gold leaves everyone believing that everyone else will accept it.

Why is gold so special?

There's another feature to a good money that will make it acceptable—that it will maintain its value. The problem with paper money is that we don't have a shortage of it. The only factors that can limit it are good sense on the part of the government and a shortage of high-quality paper—and there's ample paper and limited good sense in government. Gold is generally believed to be a good store of value because, without a revolution in reproducing heavy elements from plentiful elements, there appears to be a very limited supply. The annual output of newly mined gold is a small fraction of what already exists. And what exists is very limited. It is well known that if every ounce of gold were melted down, the total would fill only the hold of a small oil tanker—which would sink rather quickly—or the lower part of the Washington Monument. Alternatively, it would fill a cube with fifty-foot sides or a small fleet of moving vans. Since there is so little newly mined gold, people feel secure that it will remain valuable, which raises the demand, which raises the value, which so on and so on. There's no obvious *intrinsic* value of gold other than as false teeth and an electronic conductor.

When gold prices rise, gains are made by its owners and producers. The largest producers are South Africa and the Soviet Union, so when prices rise, a couple of the United States' less favorite countries make the largest gains.

What makes gold prices change?

We could have asked what makes gold prices rise, since it is frequently believed that "what goes up must come down" doesn't apply to gold, or to prices in general. I happen to think that there's reason to believe that gold prices could begin to tumble, but let's start by asking what makes them rise.

The most dramatic price increases in gold occur in anticipation of more general price increases—or, in other words, inflation—and when international crises make the movement of people and capital seem imminent. Gold price increases stemming from fears of inflation are explained by the belief that it is a good hedge against inflation. Traditionally, over very long periods of history, gold prices have kept up with other prices. The performance of real estate is mixed, and stock and equity prices have been also. Bonds often have not provided full compensation for inflation through their interest rates. This leaves gold as a better store of value than other forms of wealth. It is also an easy commodity to hold with ready marketability, judged by the small spreads between buying and selling prices. Other precious metals and gems have similar properties. If there were other inflation hedges, be assured that gold wouldn't have been so popular. For example, if inflation-indexed bonds ever come into vogue, gold would lose considerable glitter, and we could see the other side of the coin.

The effect of wars and international crises on gold stems from the ease with which refugees can take it with them. It is very difficult to move real estate in your suitcase. Financial claims, like stocks and bonds, while very easy to move, don't mean much if they're not honored, and they often lose value during wars. It *is* possible to move your intelligence and knowledge at the same time that you move your body, which perhaps explains the heavy emphasis on education in newly arrived ethnic minorities; when you're used to being moved from country to country, being a doctor, professor, engineer, accountant, or lawyer can come in handy. Nevertheless, after your training is complete, gold ownership becomes easier to achieve than additional education and is more easily converted into food and shelter.

Will gold prices always rise?

There have been periods in history when gold prices rose so much faster than other prices that people began to believe that it would always be like that. This occurred in the late 1970s. By describing what happened then, it is possible to show what could happen in the future. The story we construct could seem unlikely at this time. However, I feel that many people will be surprised.

When energy prices went through the roof, along with your heat, the largest gainers, as we well know, were the sheiks of OPEC. What do you do with so much money? While you're figuring out what the good investments are, it could be placed in gold. Then it can't be seized. Indeed, the popularity of gold in places such as the Middle East knows an extremely long history. So gold price increases due to the great energy shakedown come as no surprise.

Will things remain the same? A historical perspective shows that many periods have been dominated by certain commodities that were much in demand. During the Industrial Revolution in Britain and Germany those who owned coal earned power that eventually faded away, until it was revived very recently. Cotton gave many early American families their livelihood and prestige. Needs do change, however, and so it will be for the black gold that OPEC now owns. In many ways, changes in needs will be brought about by high prices, inducing innovations in developing alternative fuels.

Habits of consumption learned by wealthy OPEC members will be difficult to break. When we don't need the oil, how will their consumption of fine cars and other imported goods be maintained? They have purchased some technology of the 1970s to produce these goods, but this technology can quickly become obsolete unless replaced with newer technologies which will continue to be developed in countries like the United States. Current consumption levels by Middle Eastern OPEC countries will be maintained by selling their gold. If we don't want it, the price could drop dramatically.

How about returning to gold as an international money standard?

Some people think we should return to a gold standard. But just think what that means. Poor people work under very difficult conditions in South African and Russian mines to bring it out of the ground. It is then flown, under tight security, to Fort Knox and the New York Fed and places such as these, where it is again placed back in the ground. Surely we can think of better ways of spending our time.

An alternative to investing in gold is to deposit money in the bank to earn interest. These deposits include Eurodollar deposits.

What is a Eurodollar deposit?

Eurodollar deposits are an invention of the 1960s and 1970s. A Eurodollar is a bank deposit valued in U.S. dollars that is held outside of the United States. Usually it is in Europe, but it could also be in Canada, Singapore, or elsewhere. Eurodollars are part of Eurocurrencies, which are bank deposits held outside of the country that uses that particular currency. For example, a Euromark could be a bank deposit valued in deutsche marks in London, and a Eurosterling could be a deposit valued in pounds sterling in Frankfurt.

The obvious question is: Why hold dollars and other currencies in banks outside the country that uses the currency? The answer is: For convenience.

When Europeans earn dollars from selling goods or services to the United States, they could convert them into their own currencies. Sometimes, however, they know that they will need these dollars later on, perhaps in payment for what they purchase from the United States. It would be silly to convert the dollars into their own currencies only to have to reconvert them back to dollars later on. Therefore, they keep the dollars.

Of course, the Europeans could keep their dollars in a bank in the United States. This, however, would mean dealing with a bank thousands of miles away. Instead, they take their dollars, usually in the form of a check or bank draft, and leave them in a large, local bank, which could well be a European branch of a U.S. bank.

The bank in Europe doesn't allow the dollars to remain idle. It uses them in making loans to people, either in Europe or in the United States. Europeans often need dollars to make payments to Americans or even to non-Americans who want dollars. Consequently, we have European and other banks accepting and loaning dollars, and making money and profits.

How did Eurodollars orginate?

Eurodollars came about because the Soviet Union didn't want to keep dollars in the United States. In the 1960s the Soviet Union sold gold for dollars that were later needed to pay for grain purchased from Western countries. After it received dollars in exchange for gold—and before paying for the grain—it could have held the dollars in banks in the United States. However, this meant running the risk that their balances would be frozen. It also meant, in effect, making loans to capitalist banks, which have a habit, in turn, of making loans to capitalist governments. The Soviet Union instead deposited dollars in London banks, which, in turn, often loaned them to American banks and the United States government. This is only one story of the origin of Eurodollars. Another involves ceilings on interest rates.

Interest rates rose well beyond limits that U.S. banks could offer on their deposit accounts as a result of Federal Reserve regulation Q, stipulating maximum payable interest rates. American banks that still wanted dollars but couldn't offer sufficient interest to attract them opened branches abroad. These and similar branches operated by European banks weren't subject to U.S. banking regulations. Holders of dollars were happy to leave them in European banks, because Eurodollar interest rates exceeded those at home. This is a second reason for the growth of Eurodollars.

What is a petrodollar?

A petrodollar is a dollar earned from selling oil. Since oil sales generally require dollar payments, these dollars are earned from other countries as well as from the United

States. However, the other countries must first earn their dollars from the United States. This requires that the other countries have a balance of payments surplus with the United States which in turn requires that the United States is in deficit. This situation cannot continue long.

Some petrodollars are held in banks, often in Eurodollar deposit accounts. Most, however, are used for purchasing goods and services from the United States and other countries.

V

The Economists
and Their Books

16

CLASSICAL WORKS: AN ANNOTATED BIBLIOGRAPHY

I was so long writing my review that I never got around to reading the book.

Groucho Marx

Practical men, who believe themselves exempt from any intellectual influences, are usually the slaves of some defunct economist. Madmen in authority, who hear voices in the air, are distilling their frenzy from some academic scribbler of a few years back.

John Maynard Keynes

People love dropping names and titles of books they have read. Frequently the obvious implication is that just *everybody* should be familiar with what *they* know. It is very easy to feel uncomfortable when the name or title means nothing, and it does not always help to have an understanding of what is far more important than titles or authors—namely, the economic ideas and principles we have learned here. To ensure that we have sufficient familiarity with the authors and books so that we can feel completely at ease with name droppers (of people and books), we here give an annotated bibliography of the most important books and authors that a well-read person should know. We cover the classics as well as those on their way to that lofty status.

We should give credit to a noneconomist, Evan Esar,

whose 20,000 Quips and Quotes (New York: Doubleday and Co., 1968) provides humorous and even profound views on a vast range of subjects. Some of the quips and quotes used here come from this collection.

CLASSICAL ECONOMICS WORKS WELL WORTH READING

Smith, Adam. *An Inquiry into the Nature and Causes of the Wealth of Nations.* London: W. Straham and T. Caddel, 1776. Reprinted by A.M. Kelley, New York, 1966.

In *The Wealth of Nations* Smith demonstrated, by the sheer power of his arguments, the great efficiency of specialization and division of labor. This is the work for which he is most commonly remembered. He argued that by dividing labor we can develop even greater skills because of the concentrated effort we employ. In addition we become very efficient at repetitive tasks because we do not have to break our patterns of thought and activity with other tasks. Moreover, when we concentrate on a single task, it becomes easier and more worthwhile to develop tools that reduce the effort it requires. When lots of different tasks must be performed by the same person, it isn't worthwhile to expend effort to save time on just one of these many tasks. But if each of us has a single task, it can pay to take the time to find a better way.

Adam Smith illustrated the great gains in the productivity per worker from specialization and division of labor by describing the activities in a small pin factory. According to Smith, one man could produce no more than 20 pins each day when he was required to do the entire operation. When, however, the job was divided into eighteen distinct tasks, each man in a small factory was found to make an average of 4,800 pins each day. Smith argued that division of labor is limited by the size of the market. His pin factory is perhaps the most famous part of *The Wealth of Nations,* even though the book contains much more than an account of the advantages of division of labor.

Adam Smith appreciated the advantages of money in

avoiding the need to barter and believed that value was determined by the amount of labor required—not by the satisfaction given—a view no longer held. More important, he
described how the price-signals and the self-interest of seek-
ing profit could guide the economy into producing what we
all want. This is the process that is guided by the giant invisible hand.

The language of *The Wealth of Nations* is a little unfamiliar.
This has more to do with the passage of over 200 years than
with Smith's Scottish heritage. For an easier-to-read version
than the original, there is a Modern Library Edition (New
York, 1937) which contains an enlarged index, and also contains comments by Edwin Cannan and an introduction by
Max Lerner.

Before leaving Adam Smith we should mention that a
popular twentieth-century author has taken this name. His
true identity is George J. Goodman, a well-known financial
writer and editor. His major works are *The Money Game*
(New York: Random House, 1968) and *Supermoney* (New
York: Random House, 1972). *The Money Game* is an account
of random walks, behavior on Wall Street, and so on. According to Mr. Goodman, *Supermoney*, which describes the
pyramid of credit creation, was sent to a leading economist
for his review. Back came an answer that there were some
good ideas in the manuscript and that if the author wished
to develop the argument with mathematics, he might be able
to turn part of it into an academic journal article. His reply
was, "Why should I? I'll publish it in English as a book."

Ricardo, David. *Principles of Political Economy and Taxation*. 9
vols. Edited by P. Sraffa. New York: Cambridge University
Press, 1951–1952.

After Adam Smith came the great David Ricardo. A stockbroker and a self-made millionaire—when £1,000,000 sterling really meant something—Ricardo is the discoverer of
that great counterintuitive result in economics, the principle

of comparative advantage, which shows that everybody can gain from international trade. This argument is the backbone of the free-trade movement urging removal of tariffs and duties. Like Smith, Ricardo believed that the amount of labor is the chief component of value and of the price of commodities.

Mill, John Stuart. *Principles of Political Economy*. New York: The Colonial Press, 1899.

John Stuart Mill worked for the once-important British East India Company, and he strongly believed that individual liberty and freedom are best protected by the economic system that needs the least conscious direction from government. This, he convincingly argued, is the free-market, or free-enterprise, system. He was therefore very wary of big government and is, in many ways, the intellectual ancestor of Milton Friedman. He wrote numerous philosophical works on individual liberty.

Malthus, Thomas R. *An Essay on the Principle of Population or a View of Its Past and Present Effects on Human Happiness, with an Inquiry into Our Prospects Respecting the Future Removal or Mitigation of the Evils which It Occasions.* 5th ed. London: John Murray, 1817.

With a title like this, it might seem that Malthus's most popular work wouldn't need too much explanation. What else could it contain? Well, it contains an attack on the many "evils" of sex, which during a sexual revolution places him in the extreme missionary position. He believed that sex results in the severest misery, and he based his ideas on the different growth rates of the human population and the food available to feed it. He noted that population grows according to a geometrical progression—each number is the previous number *multiplied* by a constant value. For example, if each couple produces just 4 children, then from each original 2 people—of opposite sex of course—we obtain in sequence, 4, 8, 16, 32, 64, and so on. After five generations we have 64 people from our original 2 people. If each couple produces 8 children—which wasn't uncommon in Malthus's England—we have 8, 32, 128, 512, 2048, and so on, a veritable explosion of hungry mouths to feed and keep warm and happy.

While population grows geometrically, Malthus noted that because of limits on the amount of agricultural land—which seemed very limited because the potential of the Americas and Australia were not fully known—food output could grow arithmetically at best. This means each number being the previous number *plus* a constant value. For example, if output starts at 2 million tons with 2 million more tons of output each year from better farming methods, we have 2, 4, 6, 8, 10 million tons, and so on.

With population running so quickly ahead of food output, Malthus predicted famine and dreadful starvation, making twin beds absolutely mandatory. It was these dismal views by people such as Malthus that caused Thomas Carlyle, a friend of double beds, to call economics the "dismal science."

We should note that such gloomy predictions have not been the sole preserve of nineteenth-century doomsday thinkers. The Club of Rome (a club, which despite its name, we would not want to join) argued in a highly publicized book, *The Limits of Growth*, by Dennis and Donnella Meadows et al., (New York: Universe Books, 1972) that our world is becoming totally unlivable because of overpopulation and pollution and it faces a dismal future piled high with rubbish instead of Malthus's people.

Before turning to the modern economists and their works, we might mention that the early economists were prepared to offer opinions on almost everything. They did not restrict themselves to very specialized subjects as do most economists today. This was partly possible because of the lack of previous works. But, in addition, it might have been due to bravery. An advertisement reputed to have appeared in the situations-vacant section of a magazine is telling of today's economists. The advertisement stated in bold letters, WANT-ED: A ONE-HANDED ECONOMIST. In smaller print, the advertisement went on, "You might wonder why we are asking for a one-handed economist. It's because all previous economists that we have hired, when faced with an important question, have answered: 'On the one hand this could happen and on the other hand . . .' " Economists have a habit of covering every contingency. "Will stock prices go up?" they are asked. "Well, they might go up and they could come down but perhaps they'll stay the same." It might be that the economists who are good and are prepared to bet on what will happen have used their expertise to acquire wealth and they don't need to provide "advice." Nor do they need teach economics.

Marx, Karl. *Capital*. Edited by Friedrich Engels. New York: International Publishers, 1967.

The central proposition in the writings of Karl Marx in the original *Das Kapital*, published in 1867, is the exploitation of the proletariat by the capitalists. As capitalists' investment opportunities decline and they attempt to maintain profits, workers become poorer and poorer, until it pays them to revolt; the opportunity cost of the worker revolt in terms of lost income, risk to life, and such becomes less than the expected benefits. This is an inevitable development of history that produces a series of clashes between owners of capital and workers. It is more in the realm of politics and sociology than economics. This probably explains the relative shortage of Marxist economists in the United States compared to the number of Marxist sociologists, political scientists, professors of English literature, and historians.

Marxists view capital as evil. This ignores the fact that only from investment in productive machines will living standards rise. Moreover, the ownership of these machines isn't necessarily narrowly restricted to capitalists. Rather, from direct ownership of stocks or equities—or indirectly through having some holdings or interest in mutual funds or pension plans—many people are "little capitalists." If, in addition to stock ownership, life insurance, pension funds, and such we include the diversity of small businesses that remain privately owned, we find that ownership of capital in North America is remarkably well distributed.

Measures of the distribution of wealth and of income tend to show that over time there is no unavoidable tendency for things to be less equal. There certainly isn't an obvious trend toward greater misery among working people while the rich prosper. Some people attribute this to unions. This is questionable, because less than a quarter of the U.S. work force is unionized; and the same is true in Canada and in many other countries. Since it is hard to revolt against yourself, the distribution of ownership permitted by the stock market probably has more to do with defusing Marx's time bomb than unionization does.

There seem to be so many types of Marxists that you couldn't possibly be expected to know what they all might believe. With Marxist-Leninists, Marxist-Trotskyites, Marxist-Spencerists, and Marxist-Grouchoists, there's too much to know, or not to know.

This takes care of the five most notable economists of the classical variety. Next, we will discuss just five modern economists who are household words, in the better-read households.

MODERN ECONOMICS BOOKS AND AUTHORS

Marshall, Alfred. *Principles of Economics*. London: Macmillan and Co., 1890.

Although he is already a classic, it is probably fair to begin a short list of "modern" economics books and authors with Alfred Marshall's influential work. We can note that the earlier title of "political economy" has generally been reduced by Marshall's time to simply "economics," and that the focus of the economist with the deletion of "political" became that much more narrow.

Marshall clarified the analysis that lies behind the law of supply and demand and introduced a lot of new terminology and technical expertise. He is better known for his microeconomics theories and indeed provided the background material that makes up the study of microeconomics and the theory of the firm. The use of *marginal costs* and *marginal revenues* were borrowed from the work of W. Stanley Jevons (who most people remember as a marginal economist more because of the fact that he believed the trade cycle to result from sun spots—some thought he'd spent too much time in the sun) and from the work of Frenchman Léon Walras (pronounced without the *s* so that it doesn't sound like the mammal) and Austrian Karl Menger. For clarity of presentation, there are better textbooks than Marshall's *Principles*, but he deserves the credit for delineating what the newer books generally contain.

Keynes, John Maynard. *The General Theory of Employment, Interest, and Money.* London: Macmillan and Co., 1936.

The General Theory is very difficult but it is so important that it must be included in any list. This book, and its British author, have probably had more influence than any other book or economist.

Keynes is pronounced *canes* as in the candy or walking variety, not *keens*. He is also frequently called Lord Keynes, a title given him for his outstanding public service in Britain rather than for luck in ancestral heritage.

The essential principle of "Keynesian economics" (which we discussed earlier) is that only through fiscal policies of the government—taxation and spending—can full employment be maintained. Keynes therefore played down the importance of flexible prices and the money supply.

An economic idea which Keynes is famous for developing,

though not inventing, is the multiplier. This, as well as the paradox of thrift that we have described, are two key ingredients of his reliance on fiscal policy during periods of unemployment. While Keynes knew that unemployment results because real wages are too high, he also knew what could make this occur. Wages will be too high if there is a fall in aggregate demand for goods, which translates into a fall in demand for labor. He believed that declines in interest rates wouldn't always encourage investors to borrow what savers had saved because of many other things, including the *animal spirit* that affects the investor. We should note that there are almost as many versions of the Keynesian versus monetarist debate as there are people involved in it. Many economists have lost track of what ideas belong to Keynes himself and what ideas belong to his followers, the Keynesians. Axel Leijónhufvud wrote a book called *On Keynesian Economics and the Economics of Keynes: A Study in Monetary Theory* (New York: Oxford University Press, 1968). The title shows how Keynes differs from the Keynesians. In fact, Leijónhufvud has added another version of Keynesianism.

Keynes wrote a lot more than *The General Theory*. He wrote the two-volume *Treatise on Money* (London: Macmillan and Co., 1930), which would indicate that if he had lived through the post–World War II inflation, he and Friedman would have enjoyed lots of views in common. He was also part of a group that set up the international financial system that endured for a quarter of a century, even though he offered some fine ideas that were not accepted. If they had been accepted the system might have faced fewer crises. He was no fool when it came to investing on his own behalf and for his college at Cambridge University. They both became rich. He could have had a ready answer for those cheeky students who ask their economics/finance professors, "If you're so smart, how come you're not rich?" He could have just answered, "I *am* rich."

In addition to his achievements as an economist, Keynes showed enormous vitality in other activities. As a student in Cambridge he belonged to the exclusive club of intellectuals called The Apostles, and later in life he became an influential member of a similar club, the Bloomsbury Group. He married a famous ballerina. He was chairman of the National Mutual Life Insurance Company, a financial advisor to many other companies, founder of an arts theater, a noted collector of art, and an accomplished farmer. Keynes published works in probability theory and spent many years doing public service.

It is interesting to note that all but one of the economists mentioned in our review up to this point have been British. British economists were generally the most influential and important—with a few notable exceptions—well into the first half of the twentieth century.

Friedman, Milton, with the assistance of Friedman, Rose. *Capitalism and Freedom.* Chicago: University of Chicago Press, 1962.

Friedman is the leading critic of Keynes, and of just about everybody else. His essential premise is that individual liberty is the most valuable commodity and it should be protected by the economic/political system. Since Friedman believes that the individual's freedom is best protected in a world of free enterprise, he has been one of the leading champions of a *laissez-faire*, or capitalist, system. This, he believes, by hopefully preserving incentives in the form of rewards for labor and enterprise, will also result in a larger national economic product than any alternative, more highly regulated economic structure. The most complete statement of his ideas is contained in the not very long, easily readable, and highly provocative book, *Capitalism and Freedom.*

Friedman is not the first leading economist of his own time who has also been a major defender of free enterprise, but he is such a pure believer and expositor of the advantages of unregulated free markets and competition that he is constantly used as an example of the laissez-faire philosophy. So valuable is he as an example in explaining this side of economics that his long-time personal friend, Paul Samuelson, warmly remarked, "If Milton Friedman had not existed, it would have been necessary to invent him."

Friedman has argued that, contrary to the views of Keynes, monetary policy is highly effective, and indeed so effective that printing of too much money has been responsible for inflation. He supports his case with a voluminous study coauthored with Anna Schwartz, *A Monetary History of the United States, 1867–1960* (New York: National Bureau of Economic Research, 1963), and in numerous other publications. *A Monetary History* was cited as part of the reason for his receipt of the Nobel Prize in 1976—the bicentenary of America and of the publication of the *Wealth of Nations* by Adam Smith. Friedman's work in money has not been limited to the supply side. His theoretical and empirical work on the demand for money still sets the standard for modern-day research. Indeed, it is Friedman whose modernization of the quantity theory of money has made it into a theory of money demand.

Friedman believes that the Fed has so much power that it should just print, say, 4 percent more money every year and leave it at that. Anyone who isn't needed to do that can just go home, and not collect fat civil-service paychecks. It should be no surprise that Friedman is a visible part of a mass movement to trim the tax bill and thereby hopefully trim the size and level of involvement of government. Most of his energies, however, have been devoted to reviving the quantity theory of money that had become lost to most economists—except at the University of Chicago—after the publication of Keynes's *General Theory*.

Friedman's scholarship does not stop with the theory and evidence of the importance of money. He is well known for *A Theory of the Consumption Function*, a study by the National

Bureau of Economic Research, New York (Princeton: Princeton University Press, 1957) which explains the *permanent income hypothesis*. Only serious professional economists read this work on consumption. More valuable for the layman to be acquainted with for awkward social, cocktail-party and dinner-party situations are *Dollars and Deficits* (Englewood Cliffs, N.J.: Prentice Hall, 1968) and *Free to Choose* (New York: Harcourt Brace Jovanovich, 1980), which corresponds with the television show on the Public Broadcasting System of the same name. Friedman is also known for his regular contributions to *Newsweek*—a platform he has shared with Paul Samuelson.

Friedman is a statistician too, the man who designed the automatic deduction system for income taxes, which he regrets having done; and as a proponent of school vouchers, weaker federal government, and the negative income tax. He has served as advisor to several U.S. presidents and foreign governments and is considered to be, overall, a brilliant philosopher and debater.

With so much achieved—and much of it of a controversial nature—he has a huge following of admirers and many detractors too. He has never let his opponents compromise his position and for that he deserves and enjoys the respect of everyone.

Samuelson, Paul A. *Economics*. 11th ed. New York: McGraw-Hill, 1980.

Ever since the 1950s, numerous college students have been weaned on Samuelson's *Economics*, an introductory text that has gone through many revisions (perhaps partly to help ensure that successive generations of students can't buy used, older copies), and it is a very fine text indeed. Anybody who might have developed an interest in furthering his knowledge of economics could do worse than read Samuelson, or even buy a copy of his introductory textbook.

Samuelson is not only a teacher but is an economists's

economist. He has published notable papers in just about every aspect of the discipline and hardly a research topic can be approached without the researcher standing on the shoulders of the powerful Paul Samuelson. He was one of the earliest economists to apply the classical physical principles of statics and dynamics to problems in economics. This application, laid out so beautifully in his *Foundations of Economic Analysis* (Cambridge, Mass.: Harvard University Press, 1947), put economics on a new plane and has set the pattern ever since. (By the way, you might be interested to learn that Samuelson began to acquire his knowledge of mathematics and physics which he draws upon so heavily in his *Foundations*, while an undergraduate at, of all places, Friedman's longtime home, the University of Chicago.) For many years he has taught at the Massachusetts Institute of Technology.

You should be warned that *Foundations* is far from simple and is not the sort of thing you pick up while sunning yourself on the beach. It's the kind of work that requires considerable preparation and concentration. Indeed, there's a story that one day a leading American politician asked Samuelson what he should read to get an account of the developments in the world of economics since he had left college. Samuelson apparently told him to read a recent edition of his book, meaning the introductory textbook, *Economics*. By error the politician picked up *Foundations*. When the two next met, Samuelson asked the other how he had found the book. He received the reply that economics had changed so much since his day that he could no longer follow it. Don't make the same mistake.

The *Foundations of Economic Analysis* as well as dozens and dozens of highly technical, well-thought-out technical papers written over the following couple of decades earned Samuelson his well-deserved Nobel Prize. Through his many scientific contributions Samuelson has touched just about every area of study of the economist and the student of finance. His mark on the economics profession is unmistakable. He has made many important developments in multiplier-accelerator and macroeconomic theory, portfolio theory in finance, the theory of utility/satisfaction, the theory of economic growth, the theory of international trade, investment theory, populational growth and biological theory, and so on; most of them are mathematical. He is a brilliant man.

Galbraith, John Kenneth. *The Affluent Society*. 3d rev. ed. Boston: Houghton Mifflin, 1976.

Galbraith stirred the imaginations of those who considered themselves twentieth-century liberals by constructing in *The Affluent Society* what can be described as a conspiracy by business to defraud the public. The public is pictured as poor fellows in an affluent world who are duped into liking tail fins and other items, which are planned to quickly fall apart or otherwise become rapidly obsolete. With affluence already established, according to Galbraith (although those still struggling might find it hard to believe that affluence did not exist back in 1958, when the book was published), it becomes important to devote more attention to public needs than to private needs. The growth of the public sector after 1958 shows that Galbraith's desire has been realized even if he is not responsible for it. J. K. Galbraith's views place him at a great distance from Friedman, but Milton Friedman has said "Some of my best friends are Galbraithians, including John Kenneth."

In *American Capitalism: The Concept of Counterveiling Powers* (Boston: Houghton Mifflin, 1952), published four years before *The Affluent Society*, Galbraith described the power play between the mammoth units of economic conglomerates. Rather than the laissez-faire society of countless individual units coexisting in a competitive environment, Galbraith painted an alternative picture of counterveiling powers in which big business brings forth big labor and these bring forth big government. The dangers of counterveiling powers existing in a *military-industrial complex* is particularly alarming.

The giant industrial units of *American Capitalism* are the primary components of *The New Industrial State* 2d ed. (Boston: Houghton Mifflin, 1971). The goals and complexity of these monstrous units require the managerial skills of experts who collectively become a new class of *technocracy*. Galbraith sees the technostructure emerging in all societies. They staff both big business and the agent of the people responsible for checking big business—the government.

Galbraith, with a strong distrust of uncontrolled enterprise, has been a supporter of wage and price controls and other checks on business. He made his mark on at least two presidential campaigns—those of Adlai Stevenson and John F. Kennedy. He took time from his teaching career at Harvard to be United States Ambassador to India. His series on public television became a book with the same name, *The Age of Uncertainty* (Boston: Houghton Mifflin, 1977). He has authored numerous books, some of which are possibly not economics and others which are clearly not economics.

Nobody can accuse Galbraith of not trying to sniff out potential conspiracies, and there's nothing like a good conspiracy to sell an idea, and books. He can, however, be accused of not testing his conjectures as a good economic scientist should. Galbraith and fellow Canadian-born Marshall McLuhan have been described as two of the greatest Canadians that America has ever produced. Neither is great because of the scientific nature of their economics, and we could say that they have both enjoyed success from analyzing—as well as using—good advertising and promotion. They provide us with examples of the difference between what many laymen and many economists consider economics to be.

While knowing a little about the important books and authors in economics will help you survive cocktail-party and dinner-party conversations, it is much more important to understand the economic principles. Much of what has survived the testing of time and of other economists is contained in this book. If you have learned a good part of what we have explained, you will be able to appreciate exciting economic developments and to intelligently face them. But even if you forget some of what we have explained, there are still things you can do to appear highly knowledgeable. Here are some helpful tips on ways to fool people.

Obviously, you should first size up your opposition. You don't want to use fancy words at the wrong time or you might come out more bruised than if you had just retired gracefully. If you are satisfied that you can get away with it, sprinkle all discussions of economics or the economy with *model, macroeconomic policy, pace of activity, and fiscal deficit.* Be especially liberal with the word *model.* You can hardly go wrong with that.

There are a few other words that are a step beyond these. You might bravely use either *endogenous* (which means something that is explained by the model you have in mind) or *exogenous* (something *not* explained by your model). If the opposition has been drinking heavily, try *heteroscedasticity.* And if that doesn't work, let the opposition know that you believe that "we all experience homothetic preference functions and that we are therefore neutral to absolute prices, nominal incomes, and wealth." By this time you should be viewed as incomprehensibly intelligent or else as mad, which are themselves not easy to distinguish. Either way, the conversation is likely to move on to something else.

If you forget some of what you have learned about economics and if, in addition, you are too honest—or afraid—to attempt to fool people, there is still some consolation. It is not necessary that we learn every intimate detail of the working of an economy. Some details should be left for the experts, who should themselves realize the limits of what they know and of the profession they practice. Indeed, as Lord Keynes reminds us:

... in making preparations for our destiny ... let us not overestimate the importance of the economic problem. ... It is a matter for specialists—like dentistry. If economists could manage to get themselves thought of as humble, competent people, on a level with dentists, that would be splendid.

Dentists are needed when our teeth show decay from neglect, but we can prevent them from decaying. If every layman will learn what should or should not be done with the economy, as he has learned about the care of his teeth, we might help the economy avoid decay, and we could leave only the prescription of the medicine and the surgery to the professional economist.

NOTEWORTHY BOOKS

Professors of the Dismal Science, I perceive that the length of your tether is now pretty well run; and that I must request you talk a little lower in future.

Thomas Carlyle

There are some excellent books that were not mentioned, and other books that, while cited, could be avoided at small cost. This list includes books I consider noteworthy.

Dornbusch, Rudiger and Fischer, Stanley. *Macroeconomics*. 2d ed. New York: McGraw-Hill, 1980.

Friedman, Milton. *Essays in Positive Economics*. Chicago: University of Chicago Press, 1953.

_____. *Dollars and Deficits*. Englewood Cliffs, N.J.: Prentice Hall, 1968.

_____. *Free to Choose*. New York: Harcourt Brace Jovanovich, 1980.

Friedman, Milton and Schwartz, Anna Jacobson. *A Monetary History of the United States, 1867–1960*. New York: National Bureau of Economic Research, 1960.

Galbraith, John Kenneth. *The Affluent Society*. 3d rev. ed. Boston: Houghton Mifflin, 1976.

_____. *The Age of Uncertainty*. Boston: Houghton Mifflin, 1977.

Goodman, George [Adam Smith]. *The Money Game*. New York: Random House, 1968.

_____. *Supermoney*. New York: Random House, 1972.

Gordon, Robert J. *Macroeconomics.* Boston: Little, Brown and Co., 1978.

Hansen, Alvin H. *A Guide to Keynes.* New York: McGraw Hill, 1953.

Harrod, Sir Roy. *The Life of John Maynard Keynes.* New York: St. Martins, 1951.

Heilbronner, Robert. *The Worldly Philosophers: The Lives, Times and Ideas of the Great Economic Thinkers.* 5th ed. New York: Simon and Schuster, 1980.

Keynes, John Maynard. *A Treatise on Money.* London: Macmillan and Co., 1930.

————. *The General Theory of Employment, Interest and Money.* London: Macmillan and Co., 1936.

Leijönhufvud, Axel. *On Keynesian Economics and the Economics of Keynes: A Study in Monetary Theory.* New York: Oxford University Press, 1968.

Lipsey, Richard G. and Steiner, Peter O. *Economics.* 5th ed. New York: Harper and Row, 1978.

McConnell, Campbell R. *Economics.* 7th ed. New York: McGraw Hill, 1978.

Marshall, Alfred. *Principles of Economics.* London: Macmillan and Co., 1890.

Marx, Karl. *Capital.* Edited by Friedrich Engels. New York: International Publishers, 1967.

Mill, John Stuart. *Principles of Political Economy.* New York: The Colonial Press, 1899.

Ricardo, David. *Principles of Political Economy and Taxation.* 9 vols. Edited by P. Sraffa. New York: Cambridge University Press, 1951–1952.

Robinson, Joan. *Economic Philosophy: An Essay in the Progress of Economic Thought.* Garden City, N.Y.: Doubleday and Co., 1964.

Samuelson, Paul A. *Foundations of Economic Analysis.* Cambridge, Mass.: Harvard University Press, 1947.

————. *Economics.* 11th ed. New York: McGraw Hill, 1980.

————. *The Collected Scientific Papers of Paul A. Samuelson.* 4 vols. Edited by Joseph Stiglitz, Robert C. Merton, Hiroaki Nagatani and Kate Crowley. Cambridge, Mass.: MIT Press, 1966, 1972, 1966, 1978.

Smith, Adam. *An Inquiry into the Nature and Causes of the Wealth of Nations.* London: W. Straham and T. Caddel, 1776. Reprinted by A. M. Kelley, New York, 1966.

Stigler, George J. *The Theory of Price.* 3d ed. New York: Macmillan and Co., 1966.

INDEX